Astrology for Beginners

A Simple Zodiac Guide to Understand the 12 Star Signs and Unlock Self-Discovery, Personality Traits, and Compatibility

Honey Barnes

Contents

For Helena

Head on Your Shoulders
Feet on the Ground
Heart to the Stars

Introduction

In the stars, we trace the artful journey of self-discovery, illuminating our most authentic selves.

Ever wondered why your bestie, a fiery Aries, is always up for an adventure while your cool-as-a-cucumber Libra sibling prefers a calm evening with a good book? Or you've pondered why your organizational skills as a Virgo make you the go-to planner in your group. Welcome to "Astrology for Beginners: A Simple Zodiac Guide to Understand the 12 Star Signs and Unlock Self-Discovery, Personality Traits, and Compatibility." This isn't just a book; it's your cosmic roadmap, a fun-filled journey through the stars designed to help you discover the celestial secrets behind your personality, relationships, and much more.

Our journey into astrology began with a spark of curiosity and has grown into a comprehensive exploration of how the stars can shed light on our unique personalities, strengths, weaknesses, and how we interact with the world and others. This book is a culmination of that exploration, offering insights and guidance into the enchanting world of astrology. It's designed to share the magic and wisdom of the stars, inviting you on an adventure of self-discovery and cosmic understanding.

So, what's in store for you in these pages? Picture this: a friendly chat with a knowledgeable friend here to demystify the world of astrology. We're keeping it simple, engaging, and oh-so-relatable. You'll get to know each of the 12 zodiac signs intimately – not just their essential traits but the nitty-gritty of what makes each sign tick. You'll dive into the elements and modalities that shape these signs, adding layers to your understanding.

But it's not just about knowing your sign. This book is about connection – how your sign influences your relationships. Ever wondered why you click instantly with some people but clash with others? We'll explore love, friendship, and even work relationships through the lens of the zodiac, giving you insights that might make you go, "Aha, now I get it!"

And here's the cherry on top: you'll learn how to apply this knowledge practically. Whether it's harnessing your strengths, navigating your weaknesses, or understanding your friends, family, or love interests better, this book has got you covered.

But, we promise, no astro-babble here. We're keeping it light, fun, and super easy to grasp. Think of this as Astrology 101 – the course you never knew you needed but will be glad you took.

As we embark on this journey together, remember that astrology is a tool for self-discovery, not a one-size-fits-all solution. It's about exploring possibilities, understanding potential, and having a bit of fun along the way. So, keep an open mind and a curious heart, and get ready to unlock the secrets of the stars.

Next up, we dive into the world of the zodiac. Get ready to meet Aries, the energetic pioneer; Taurus, the sensual stabilizer; Gemini, the curious communicator; and all the other fascinating signs that make up our astrological tapestry. Let's turn the page and start exploring the stars!

Chapter 1
THE ZODIAC

The zodiac holds the map to our souls, revealing the magic woven into our very being.

Brief Definition of the Zodiac

L et's kick off our zodiac journey with a quick and easy definition to set the stage. Picture the zodiac as a cosmic GPS, mapping out the sky and giving us a stellar script on personality traits and life paths. The term 'zodiac' itself has a bit of star-studded history. It comes from the Greek word 'zodiakos', meaning 'circle of animals'. Think of it as an imaginary belt in the sky, stretching about eight degrees north and south of the ecliptic – the path the sun takes across the sky over the course of a year.

This celestial belt is divided into twelve equal parts, each corresponding to a constellation. These are the twelve zodiac signs that we talk about – Aries, Taurus, Gemini, and so on, right up to Pisces. Each segment, or sign, covers about 30 degrees of the celestial longitude and is named after the constellation it originally corresponded with. The division into twelve is significant because it roughly corresponds to the lunar months in a year.

The fascinating bit? These signs don't just randomly exist. They're anchored to Earth's yearly orbit around the sun. As we orbit, the sun appears to pass through these signs. It's like a cosmic backdrop to the sun's path, and it plays a huge role in what we call 'sun-sign astrology' – the kind you read in your daily horoscope.

But here's a little twist: the constellations have shifted over time due to the Earth's wobble on its axis, a phenomenon known as precession. So, the zodiac signs as we know them in astrology don't perfectly align with the actual constellations anymore. But worry not! Astrologers stick to the 'tropical zodiac', which is based on the seasons and the sun's position at the vernal equinox, keeping our astrological signs consistent through time.

In a nutshell, the zodiac is this marvelous, mystical belt in the sky that tells a story about who we are, how we love, and how we dance through life. It's the starting block of astrology, a guide to understanding ourselves and the people around us.

The Circle of Animals: Origins and Meaning

Now, let's talk about the heart and soul of the zodiac – the Circle of Animals. This isn't just any circle; it's a starry ring filled with tales and symbolism, a cosmic carousel of animal and human figures that have fascinated humanity for ages.

The term "Circle of Animals" directly relates to the Greek origin of 'zodiac', or 'zodiakos', literally translating to 'circle of animals'. This name is a nod to the majority of the zodiac signs being represented by creatures, both real and mythical. For instance, Leo the lion, Taurus the bull, and Scorpio the scorpion. It's like a celestial zoo, each animal embodying the traits and qualities of its corresponding sign.

But where did this concept originate? The zodiac's roots can be traced back to ancient Babylonian astrology, later adopted by the Greeks. These civilizations observed the sky, charting stars and constellations, and over time, they connected these celestial patterns with seasons, mythology, and their gods. Each zodiac sign, represented by an animal or a human figure, was infused with mythological stories and meanings, reflecting the beliefs and cultures of these ancient peoples.

For example, Aries is associated with the story of the Golden Ram in Greek mythology, while Cancer is linked to the giant crab that Hera sent to fight Hercules. These stories were more than just tales; they were ways to explain the natural world and human nature.

The Circle of Animals isn't just a collection of constellations; it's a symbolic representation of life's cyclical nature. Each animal sign symbolizes different personality traits, strengths, weaknesses, and destinies. They serve as a mirror to our human experiences, reflecting our journey through life – from the impulsive energy of Aries, the first sign, to the wise, mystical Pisces, the last.

This circle is also a testament to our ancestors' connection to the natural world and the skies. They didn't just see patterns in the stars; they saw stories, lessons, and a deeper understanding of themselves and the universe.

In essence, the Circle of Animals is a blend of astronomy, mythology, and symbolism. It's a guide that has been used for centuries to explore human behavior, predict futures, and navigate the complexities of existence. As we journey through each sign in the upcoming chapters, we'll uncover the unique stories and meanings behind these celestial creatures and figures.

The Zodiac Calendar

As we continue our celestial journey, let's dive into the Zodiac Calendar, a crucial part of understanding astrology. This isn't your typical calendar hanging on the wall; it's a cosmic schedule, mapping out the sun's path through the zodiac signs over the course of a year.

The Zodiac Calendar is based on the sun's apparent movement through the twelve zodiac signs. Each sign occupies a month-like period when the sun is aligned with the corresponding constellation (at least, traditionally). The calendar kicks off with the vernal equinox, typically around March 21st, marking the beginning of the astrological year with Aries.

Here's a quick guide to the star signs and their date ranges:

- Aries (March 21 - April 19): The initiator, the fiery starter of the zodiac.
- Taurus (April 20 - May 20): The steadfast, sensual earth sign that loves stability.
- Gemini (May 21 - June 20): The communicative, dual-natured air sign.
- Cancer (June 21 - July 22): The nurturing, emotional water sign.
- Leo (July 23 - August 22): The dramatic, sunny, and confident fire sign.
- Virgo (August 23 - September 22): The meticulous, service-oriented earth sign.
- Libra (September 23 - October 22): The balanced, harmonious air sign.
- Scorpio (October 23 - November 21): The intense, mysterious water sign.
- Sagittarius (November 22 - December 21): The adventurous, philosophical fire sign.
- Capricorn (December 22 - January 19): The ambitious, disciplined earth sign.
- Aquarius (January 20 - February 18): The innovative, humanitarian air sign.
- Pisces (February 19 - March 20): The dreamy, empathetic water sign.

It's important to note that these dates can vary slightly depending on the year and your location. The sun doesn't switch signs at midnight sharp, so if you're born on the cusp (the transition between signs), you might want to check an ephemeris or consult an astrologer to know your sun sign for sure.

The Zodiac Calendar is more than just dates and signs; it's a symbol of the cyclical nature of life and the universe. Each sign brings its own energy, challenges, and opportunities. As we journey through the calendar in the upcoming chapters, you'll get to explore the unique qualities and quirks of each sign, painting a vivid picture of the astrological year.

Chapter 2
ELEMENTS & MODALITIES

Elements and modalities weave the cosmic tapestry of our individual essence, shaping our journey through the stars.

Welcome to Chapter 3, where we dive into the elements and modalities of astrology – the secret sauce that adds flavor to each zodiac sign. Understanding these concepts is like getting the key to a treasure chest; it unlocks a deeper comprehension of the star signs and how they interact with the world. So, let's break it down and get ready to transition into the fascinating world of each star sign.

The Elements

Fire

First up, the Fire signs: Aries, Leo, and Sagittarius. Imagine a crackling fire – dynamic, warm, and impossible to ignore. That's the essence of Fire signs. They're the go-getters, the trailblazers, full of passion and energy. Think of the enthusiasm of Aries, the confidence of Leo, and the adventurous spirit of Sagittarius. Fire signs are all about action and inspiration, but they can also be impulsive and quick-tempered. In their chapters, we'll explore how this fiery energy fuels their personalities and relationships.

Earth

Next, we have the Earth signs: Taurus, Virgo, and Capricorn. Solid and reliable like the ground we stand on, Earth signs are the stabilizers of the zodiac. They value security, practicality, and results. Taurus brings a love for life's earthly pleasures, Virgo offers meticulous attention to detail, and Capricorn embodies discipline and ambition. Earth signs, however, can sometimes be too rigid or materialistic. We'll dig deeper into their grounding energy in their respective chapters.

Air

Then there's Air: Gemini, Libra, and Aquarius. Think of a breeze – always moving, refreshing, and vital. Air signs are the thinkers and communicators of the zodiac. They're intellectual, curious, and sociable. Gemini sparkles with wit, Libra seeks balance and harmony, and Aquarius brings innovative ideas. But Air signs can also be aloof and indecisive. In their chapters, we'll see how this airy energy influences their approach to life and interactions.

Water

Finally, the Water signs: Cancer, Scorpio, and Pisces. Like the ocean, they're deep, emotional, and mysterious. Water signs are intuitive and sensitive, often possessing a strong creative and spiritual side. Cancer is nurturing, Scorpio is intense and passionate, and Pisces is dreamy and empathetic. However, Water signs can also get lost in their emotions or become overly secretive. We'll explore the depths of their emotional oceans in their chapters.

The Modalities

Cardinal

Moving onto the modalities, let's start with Cardinal signs: Aries, Cancer, Libra, and Capricorn. These are the initiators, the leaders. They're great at starting projects and pioneering new ideas. However, they can sometimes struggle with follow-through.

Fixed

Fixed signs – Taurus, Leo, Scorpio, and Aquarius – are the stabilizers. Once they set their mind on something, they're in it for the long haul. They're reliable and determined, but can also be stubborn and resistant to change.

Mutable

And lastly, Mutable signs: Gemini, Virgo, Sagittarius, and Pisces. These are the flexible, adaptable signs. They're great at adjusting to change and finishing what was started. But, they can sometimes be perceived as inconsistent or indecisive.

Understanding these elements and modalities is crucial as we delve into the personality traits and compatibility of each star sign. They add layers and depth to our astrological profiles, offering a richer understanding of ourselves and others. As we transition into the following chapters, keep these concepts in mind – they're the threads that weave together the tapestry of the zodiac.

Chapter 3
ARIES

In the heart of an Aries, you'll find the soul of a knight, the curiosity of a cat, and occasionally, the attention span of a goldfish.

W e begin our journey in the dynamic world of Aries, the zodiac's trailblazer and initiator. In this chapter, we delve into the fiery essence of Aries, the first sign in the astrological cycle. Known for their boldness, energy, and pioneering spirit, Aries individuals embody courage and determination. Whether you are an Aries yourself or simply seeking to understand the Aries in your life, this chapter promises to be an enlightening exploration. We'll uncover the unique characteristics that define this spirited fire sign, from their natural leadership qualities to their zest for life. Let's begin our exploration into the vibrant and energetic world of Aries.

Zodiac Birth Dates

March 21 - April 19: Aries season is like the start of a great party – full of energy and excitement. If you're born in this window, congrats, you're officially an Aries!

Core Attributes

- **Ruling Planet:** Mars, the red-hot planet all about action and oomph!
- **Element:** Fire, because Aries folks are constantly burning with enthusiasm.
- **Symbol-The Ram:** Stubborn, strong, and not afraid to butt heads.

When it comes to Aries, think bold, fiery, and unstoppable! Born under the ruling planet Mars, named after the Roman god of war, Aries folks are natural-born leaders with a dash of warrior spirit. They're the zodiac's fearless trailblazers, always ready to dive headlong into even the most challenging situations. Imagine a mix of determination and a go-getter attitude that's as fiery as their element, Fire. They have this inner flame that keeps them warm, driven, and always raring to go.

Aries is symbolized by the Ram, and let me tell you, it couldn't be more fitting. Like their animal counterpart, Aries folks have this incredible ability to push forward, no matter what. Stubborn? A little. But it's more about their unwavering focus and determination. They're not the ones to back down from a challenge; they're at the front of the line, ready to take charge and make things happen.

And let's remember their energy. If you've ever met an Aries, you know they're all about that vibrant, infectious enthusiasm. They're the ones with the spark in their eyes, always up for a new adventure or a fresh challenge. It's this zest for life that makes Aries so compelling and charismatic. They're not just living life; they're grabbing it by the horns and steering it wherever they want it to go.

So, in a nutshell, Aries is your go-to when you need someone bold, brimming with energy, and unafraid to blaze new trails. They're the zodiac's pioneers, always a few steps ahead, leading the way with their fiery spirit and fearless heart.

Personality Traits

- **Energetic and Bold:** Aries, you're the human equivalent of a double espresso shot – always ready to go!
- **Confident:** You walk into a room, and people notice. It's like wearing an invisible crown.
- **Adventurous:** For Aries, life's a daring adventure or nothing at all.

Diving into the personality traits of Aries, you're entering a realm of dynamic and spirited individuals who are as lively as they are determined. An Aries walks into a room, and you can't help but feel their presence; they radiate this energetic vibe that's both exciting and a tad overwhelming. They embody the phrase 'living life to the fullest,' always looking for the next big thing, adventure, or challenge to conquer.

At the heart of an Aries personality is an unyielding courage and confidence that's both admirable and infectious. They're the ones who aren't afraid to take risks, push their boundaries, and be the first to try something new. This fearless approach often makes them pioneers, always a step ahead in trying new things or spearheading initiatives. Aries are not deterred by setbacks; they use them as building blocks to achievement and growth.

But it's not all about being bold and brash. Aries have a particular childlike enthusiasm and genuine curiosity about the world, making them incredibly endearing. They approach life with a sense of wonder, always eager to learn, see, and do more. This zest for life is contagious, often inspiring those around them to live a little more boldly and freely.

However, Aries can sometimes be too headstrong for their own good. Their 'act first, think later' mantra can lead them into tricky situations. Their impulsive nature means they often make decisions on the fly without fully considering the consequences. It's part of their charm, but it can also be frustrating for those more cautious and considered.

Essentially, Aries is like the spark that ignites a flame – full of potential, energy, and the power to initiate change. They bring excitement and boldness to everything they do, often leading the way with their courageous and enthusiastic spirit.

Innate Strengths

- **Leadership:** You're rallying the troops, whether planning a trip or spearheading a project.
- **Independence:** Aries doesn't wait for things to happen. You make them happen!
- **Positivity:** Your glass? Always half full. Your spirit? Unbreakable.

The strengths of Aries are as vibrant and dynamic as their personality. At the forefront is their leadership ability. An Aries doesn't just lead; they inspire. With their natural confidence and can-do attitude, they have this unique way of rallying others around a cause or an idea. They're the ones people look to when a situation calls for someone fearless and willing to take charge. Whether leading a project at work or planning an epic road trip, Aries is your go-to leader.

Then there's their independence. Aries are fiercely self-reliant. They don't wait for things to happen; they make them happen. This quality is not just about being alone; it's about their strong sense of self and the confidence to pursue what they want on their terms. This level of independence means they're often ahead of the curve, breaking new ground and setting trends.

Another significant strength is their positivity. Aries has an infectious enthusiasm that brightens up any room. They see the glass as half full, and their optimism can be a beacon of light in challenging times. This positive outlook isn't just about being happy; it's a source of strength that helps them (and those around them) to push through challenging situations. This unwavering positivity often helps them achieve their goals and inspires others to do the same.

What's truly remarkable about Aries is their ability to bounce back from setbacks. They're not ones to wallow in self-pity or give up when the going gets tough. Instead, they use challenges as fuel to come back stronger and more determined. This resilience is a hallmark of their character, making them capable of overcoming almost anything life throws them.

In summary, Aries' strengths lie in their leadership qualities, independence, positivity, and resilience. These traits make them not only formidable individuals but also inspiring figures who have the power to motivate and energize those around them.

Challenges to Overcome

- **Impulsiveness:** Sometimes, you leap before you look. Skydiving, yes. Think twice about decisions, maybe?
- **Impatience:** Waiting isn't your strong suit. Slow internet? Long lines? No, thank you!
- **Competitive:** It's great to win, but not everything's a race.

While Aries possesses many strengths, like all signs, they also have weaknesses. One of the most prominent is their impulsive nature. Aries is known for acting first and thinking later. This spontaneity can sometimes lead to thrilling adventures. Still, it can also result in hasty decisions or actions they might later regret. Their impulsiveness can be both a source of excitement and a cause for caution, as it often means they jump into situations without fully considering the consequences.

Another challenge lies in their impatience. Aries individuals are not fans of waiting around. They crave immediate results and can become easily frustrated when things don't move at their preferred fast pace. This impatience can be challenging in situations requiring a more measured, long-term approach, and they might struggle in scenarios where patience is vital.

Competitiveness is another double-edged sword for Aries. While it drives them to achieve great things, excessive competitiveness can lead to stress and conflict. They love to be the best and often view life as a series of competitions. This trait, while motivating, can sometimes alienate others or lead to an unhealthy fixation on winning at all costs.

Lastly, Aries can be headstrong and stubborn. Once they've decided something, it can be challenging to change their course. This determination is admirable but can also manifest as a refusal to consider alternative viewpoints or solutions. Their strong will is a powerful asset, but it can become a hindrance when flexibility and adaptability are required.

The challenges of Aries – impulsiveness, impatience, competitive-ness, and stubbornness – are often the flip sides of their strengths. These traits can lead to incredible achievements and moments of joy. Still, they can also pose challenges in certain situations and relationships.

Relationship Dynamics in Love and Friendship

- **Ideal Partner**: Best with signs that can handle your fiery nature – think Leo, Sagittarius, or even a grounded Libra.
- **Friendship Dynamics:** You need pals who love your energy but can also tell you to cool your jets when needed.

Aries, marked by their fiery essence and zest for life, approach love and friendship with passion, loyalty, and an adventurous spirit. In the landscape of personal relationships, they seek connections that resonate with their vibrant energy and match their enthusiasm for life's adventures.

In romantic relationships, Aries are known for their bold and passionate approach. They are drawn to the excitement of the chase and often fall for partners who can engage in this dance of dynamic and spirited romance. Aries in love is a blend of spontaneity, passion, and an unwavering dedication to their partner. They flourish with signs that keep pace with their energy and bring a harmonizing influence.

When it comes to friendships, Aries is the embodiment of loyalty and enthusiasm. They are friends who are always ready for new adventures and are dependable in times of need. However, their competitive nature and zest for action are best matched with friends who can join in the fun or offer a calming counterpoint.

Most Compatible Signs with Aries:

Leo: This Fire sign duo shines brightly with a shared love for excitement and the dramatic. Aries and Leo thrive together due to their mutual understanding of each other's need for independence and admiration. Their relationship is marked by passion, respect, and a joyous celebration of life's grandeur.

Sagittarius: Sagittarius pairs wonderfully with Aries, as both signs are eager for adventure and boast a positive outlook on life. This pairing is successful because of their mutual desire for exploration and new experiences. Together, they embark on life's journey with enthusiasm and an unquenchable thirst for adventure.

Gemini: Air sign Gemini is complementary to Aries' fiery nature. This pairing is booming due to Gemini's intellectual curiosity and Aries' action-oriented approach. Together, they create a relationship that is intellectually stimulating, lively, and full of diverse experiences.

Aquarius: Aquarius uniquely matches Aries, blending intellectual engagement with a shared desire for independence and excitement. This relationship flourishes on mutual respect for each other's individuality and a shared vision of future possibilities.

Aries find fulfilling relationships with signs that share their enthusiasm for life, offer intellectual stimulation, and understand their need for independence. Their ideal partnerships balance their fiery nature with harmony and mutual respect.

Career Insights

- **Career Path:** Anything fast-paced – think entrepreneur, athlete, or firefighter.
- **In the Workplace:** You're the one who gets things done, but remember, teamwork makes the dream work.
- **Career Tips:** Channel that Aries fire into positive energy, and you're unstoppable!

Aries, characterized by their dynamic energy and leadership qualities, brings a bold and pioneering spirit to the workplace. In their professional life, Aries is driven by challenges, a desire for independence, and an innate ability to take initiative. Their approach to work is often marked by enthusiasm, a competitive edge, and a preference for taking the lead.

One of Aries' greatest strengths in their career is their fearless approach to challenges. They are bold in taking risks or venturing into new territories. This makes them excellent leaders and innovators, always ready to blaze new trails and inspire their teams with courage and decisiveness.

Their natural leadership qualities are another significant asset. Aries possesses a clear vision and the ability to motivate others, making them effective in roles where leadership and direction are required. Their energy and passion can be infectious, often rallying their colleagues to work towards common goals with vigor and enthusiasm.

However, Aries may sometimes need help with patience and attention to detail. Their eagerness to move forward and achieve results quickly can sometimes lead to overlooking finer points. Balancing their fast-paced approach with a mindfulness of details can enhance their effectiveness.

Most Suitable Work/Career Choices for Aries:

Entrepreneurship: Aries' natural leadership skills and love for challenges make entrepreneurship an ideal career path. Their ability to start initiatives and drive projects forward is critical in entrepreneurship, where taking risks and innovating are crucial.

Management and Leadership Roles: Aries thrives in positions of leadership. Whether in corporate, nonprofit, or public sectors, their ability to lead, motivate, and make decisive choices makes them successful managers and directors.

Sales and Marketing: The dynamic and competitive nature of sales and marketing aligns well with Aries' spirited and persuasive communication skills. Their energy and drive can be highly effective in these roles, pushing them to excel in reaching targets and winning clients.

Emergency Services: Careers in emergency services, such as firefighting, law enforcement, or emergency medical services, suit Aries' desire for action and ability to respond swiftly and decisively in high-pressure situations.

Sports and Physical Training: Aries' energy and competitive spirit make them well-suited for careers in sports, whether as athletes, coaches, or personal trainers. Their drive to excel and push physical limits aligns perfectly with the demands of sports and fitness careers.

Aries excels in work environments that offer challenges, opportunities for leadership, and a dynamic pace. They are most successful in careers that allow them to utilize their initiative-taking nature, leadership abilities, and love for competition.

Famous Aries Personalities

- **Emma Watson:** Beauty, brains, and a dash of Aries boldness.
- **Robert Downey Jr.:** The Iron Man himself – charming, witty, and a true Aries at heart.
- **Lady Gaga:** The queen of reinvention, fierce and fabulously Aries.

So there you have it – Aries in a nutshell. You're dynamic and determined, and you know how to make life an adventure. Keep being awesome, Aries!

Chapter 4
TAURUS

Master of comfort, collector of fine things, and a believer in the art of napping.

W elcome to the world of Taurus, the steadfast and serene sign of the zodiac. If you're a Taurus, get ready to nod in agreement; if not, prepare to understand the Taureans in your life like never before. As we shift gears from the fiery Aries to the earthy Taurus, we enter a realm of calm, comfort, and a love for life's pleasures. Known for their practicality, loyalty, and love for all things beautiful, Taureans are the zodiac's embodiment of persistence and grace. So, let's take a leisurely stroll through the meadows of Taurus traits, uncovering what makes these gentle bulls the bedrock of stability and sensuality in the astrological universe.

Zodiac Birth Dates

April 20 - May 20: Taurus season shifts from Aries's fiery energy to the more grounded, sensual rhythms of the Bull.

Core Attributes

- **Ruling Planet:** Venus, a star of love and beauty, influences Taurus' appreciation for the finer things in life.
- **Element:** Earth, which explains their grounded and practical nature.
- **Symbol-The Bull**: Symbolic of strength, stability, and quiet determination.

When you think Taurus, think stability, serenity, and a touch of indulgence. Born under Venus, the planet of love and beauty, Taureans have a natural affinity for the finer things in life. They revel in sensory experiences, whether sumptuous food, beautiful art, or the simple pleasure of a soft blanket. This Venusian influence also lends them a certain charm and a keen eye for aesthetics.

In terms of their element, Taurus is as grounded as they come. As an Earth sign, they're practical, reliable, and down-to-earth. They're the folks you count on, with their feet firmly planted on the ground. This earthiness also gives them a remarkable sense of calm, making them a soothing presence in any chaotic situation.

Symbolized by the Bull, Taureans embody this creature's strength and stubbornness. There's a quiet power to a Taurus, a resilient force that doesn't need to boast or brag. They're persistent, often quietly working towards their goals until they achieve them. But, much like the Bull, once they've made up their mind, it's hard to sway them. This can be both a strength and a challenge, as we'll see in the upcoming sections.

The critical characteristics of Taurus blend the beauty of Venus with the stability of Earth, creating individuals who are not just dependable and practical but also appreciate beauty and comfort in all its forms.

Personality Traits

- **Calm and Methodical:** Unlike the impulsive Aries, Taurus takes a more measured approach to life, valuing stability and routine.
- **Patient and Reliable:** A Taurus is someone you can count on, always there when you need them, and incredibly patient.
- **Lover of Comfort:** They appreciate comfort and luxury, often seen in their love for good food, nice things, and cozy environments.

Diving into the personality traits of Taurus, you'll find a fascinating mix of calm resilience and a love for life's simple pleasures.

Taureans are known for their tranquil demeanor, often serving as a grounding force amid chaos. They approach life with a steady pace, preferring stability over chaos and consistency over change. This makes them incredibly reliable – if a Taurus says they'll do something, you can bet it'll be done.

But there's more to Taurus than just their steadfast nature. They have a deep appreciation for beauty and sensory experiences. This love for the finer things isn't about extravagance but savoring the world's textures, flavors, and colors. A Taurus takes pleasure in the small things – a good meal, a beautiful sunset, the feel of luxurious fabric. They remind us to slow down and appreciate the here and now.

Another notable trait of Taurus is their patience. They understand that good things take time and are willing to wait. This patience is a superpower in a world that's always rushing. It allows them to see projects through to completion and stand by people and ideas they believe in.

However, Taureans can also be creatures of habit. They find comfort in routine and familiarity, sometimes to the point of becoming resistant to change. They prefer the known path to uncharted territory, which can sometimes limit their experiences and growth.

In relationships, Taurus individuals are loyal and devoted. They value deep, meaningful connections and are often the stabilizing force in their relationships. But their need for stability can sometimes translate into possessiveness or a tendency to stay in situations longer than they should.

In essence, Taureans are like the roots of a tree – grounded, nurturing, and stable, providing support and beauty, but sometimes a bit too fixed in their place.

Innate Strengths

- **Practicality:** Taurus is the zodiac's practical planner, always thinking ahead and making well-thought-out decisions.
- **Loyalty:** Once a Taurus is your friend, they're your friend for life. Their loyalty knows no bounds.
- **Persistence:** A Taurus might take a while to get going, but once they do, they are unstoppable. Their tenacity is legendary.

The strengths of a Taurus are deeply rooted in their earthy nature, providing a solid foundation in their personal and professional lives. First and foremost, their practicality shines through in everything they do. Taureans have a no-nonsense approach to life; they're realistic, pragmatic, and not prone to fanciful thinking. This practical mindset makes them excellent problem solvers, capable of finding tangible solutions to complex issues.

Another significant strength is their reliability. If you need someone you can count on, look no further than a Taurus. They are steadfast and loyal, often the ones friends and family turn to in need. Their word is their bond, and they take their commitments seriously, whether in their personal relationships or professional responsibilities.

Patience is yet another hallmark of Taurus's strength. They under-stand that some of the best things in life take time to develop, and they're more than willing to wait. This patience extends to their personal growth, relationships, and career ambitions. It allows them to cultivate and nurture projects and relationships, leading to deep and meaningful outcomes.

Persistence is also a key strength. Much like the symbol of the Bull, Taureans set their sights on a goal and persist until they achieve it. They're not deterred by setbacks or challenges but view them as opportunities to learn and grow. This persistent nature ensures they often achieve what they want, even if it takes longer than expected.

Lastly, Taureans sincerely appreciate beauty and comfort, which can be a strength. This appreciation leads them to create harmonious and aesthetically pleasing environments at home and work. It also makes them adept at professions involving art, design, and anything requiring a keen eye for aesthetics.

The strengths of Taurus – practicality, reliability, patience, persistence, and an appreciation for beauty – make them well-rounded and dependable individuals valued in their personal circles and professional environments.

Challenges to Overcome

- **Stubbornness:** The Bull can be incredibly stubborn, often seen as sticking to their ways and resisting change.
- **Materialistic Tendencies:** Their love for the finer things can sometimes lead to materialism.
- **Comfort Zone:** Taurus can be too comfortable sometimes, leading to complacency and resistance to new experiences.

While Taurus boasts many strengths, they also have their share of weaknesses. One of the most prominent is their stubbornness. Symbolized by the Bull, Taureans can be incredibly headstrong, often sticking to their ways and resisting change. This can be both a strength and a weakness. At the same time, it shows their commitment and reliability; it can also make them inflexible and resistant to necessary changes.

Another weakness lies in their comfort-seeking nature. Taureans love comfort and luxury, sometimes to the point of indulgence. They can be materialistic, valuing physical possessions and luxuries, and may struggle when these are absent. Their love for comfort can also lead to complacency, where they become too settled in their ways, avoiding risks or challenges that could lead to growth.

Additionally, Taureans' resistance to change can manifest as a fear of the unknown, making them overly cautious or hesitant to try new things. This can limit their experiences and prevent them from seizing opportunities that require stepping out of their comfort zone.

Lastly, their need for security and stability can sometimes become possessive, particularly in relationships. They can be overly protective or controlling, fearing any threat to their cherished stability. This can strain relationships unless balanced with trust and understanding.

Taurus's challenges – stubbornness, a tendency toward materialism and comfort, resistance to change, and possessiveness – are the flip side of their strengths. Recognizing and addressing these weaknesses can help Taureans find a more balanced and fulfilling approach to life.

Relationship Dynamics in Love and Friendship

- **Ideal Partners:** Earth signs like Virgo and Capricorn understand Taurus' need for stability. In contrast, Water signs like Cancer and Pisces bring emotional depth to the relationship.

- **Friendship Dynamics:** Taurus makes a loyal and dependable friend, though their stubbornness can sometimes be a hurdle.

Taurus, the embodiment of steadfastness and sensuality, navigates love and friendship with a blend of loyalty, warmth, and a preference for stability. In their personal relationships, Taurus seeks connections that resonate with their deep appreciation for comfort, reliability, and the finer things in life.

In romantic relationships, Taurus is known for their earthy and nurturing approach. They value stability and security, often seeking partners who share their desire for a harmonious and comfortable life. In love, a Taurus is intensely loyal, affectionate, and committed. They thrive in relationships that offer them a sense of security and appreciation for the sensual pleasures of life. Their ideal partners are those who can appreciate everyday beauty and understand the importance of building a solid foundation for the future.

When it comes to friendships, Taurus is a reliable friend. They value long-term relationships built on shared values and trust. Their friends appreciate their practical advice, unwavering support, and occasional indulgence in life's luxuries. Taurus enjoys friendships that are grounded, genuine, and devoid of drama.

Most Compatible Signs with Taurus:

Virgo: Both Earth signs, Taurus and Virgo, share a practical approach to life and love. This pairing is successful because of their mutual understanding of the need for stability and routine. They appreciate each other's attention to detail and the comfort of a well-organized life.

Capricorn: Capricorn complements Taurus's desire for stability with their ambition and discipline. This relationship is built on a foundation of mutual respect and shared goals. Together, they create an ambitious and grounded partnership, balancing Taurus's love for comfort with Capricorn's drive for success.

Cancer: Water sign Cancer offers emotional depth and nurturing, harmonizing well with Taurus's need for security and comfort. This relationship flourishes due to their shared values of loyalty, family, and the desire to create a harmonious home life.

Pisces: Pisces brings a touch of romance and imagination to the grounded nature of Taurus. This pairing is successful because Pisces adds emotional depth and creativity, complementing Taurus's practicality and love for beauty.

Taurus finds the most fulfilling relationships with signs of stability, practicality, and emotional depth. Their ideal partnerships provide a sense of security, shared values, and an appreciation for life's simple yet profound pleasures.

Career Insights

- **Career Path:** Taurus excels in careers that allow them to use their practical skills and appreciate their need for a stable, routine-based environment.

- **In the Workplace:** They are reliable and hardworking, often the backbone of their team.
- **Career Tips:** Embrace flexibility and be open to change to avoid stagnation.

Taurus, known for their practicality, steadfastness, and appreciation for stability, bring a grounded and systematic approach to their professional life. In their career, Taurus values consistency, security, and the opportunity to utilize their strong work ethic and attention to detail. Their approach to work is characterized by patience, reliability, and a preference for well-structured environments.

One of Taurus' greatest strengths in their career is their persistence and dedication. They can sustain effort and hard work, making them reliable employees or team members. This steady approach often leads to high-quality results and a reputation for trustworthiness and consistency in their work.

Their practical and methodical nature is another significant asset. Taurus excels in roles that require careful planning and attention to detail. They have a natural ability to manage resources efficiently, whether time, money, or materials, making them effective in roles that require practical and tangible outcomes.

However, Taurus may sometimes struggle with adaptability and embracing rapid change. Their preference for stability and routine can sometimes limit their flexibility. Balancing their need for consistency and willingness to adapt can enhance their effectiveness in a rapidly changing work environment.

Most Suitable Work/Career Choices for Taurus:

Finance and Accounting: Taurus' methodical nature and practical approach make them well-suited for careers in finance and accounting. Their reliability and attention to detail are assets in managing financial resources and ensuring accuracy in financial matters.

Architecture and Design: The combination of Taurus' artistic sensibility and practical skills aligns well with careers in architecture and design. Their ability to balance aesthetic appeal with functional design makes them effective in these creative yet practical fields.

Gardening and Landscaping: Taurus' connection to the Earth and love for nature can lead them to find fulfillment in gardening, landscaping, or agricultural work. Their patience and nurturing approach are well-suited to careers that involve working with plants and the natural environment.

Culinary Arts: Taurus' appreciation for sensory experiences and attention to detail can make them successful in the culinary arts. Whether as chefs or pastry artists, they excel in creating delicious and aesthetically pleasing culinary creations.

Management in Stable Industries: Taurus thrives in management roles within industries that offer stability and gradual growth. Their practical approach and steady leadership style are effective in sectors where consistency and long-term planning are valued.

Taurus excels in work environments that offer stability, practical challenges, and the opportunity to apply their systematic approach. They are most successful in careers that allow them to utilize their practical skills, steady work ethic, and appreciation for tangible results.

Famous Taurus Personalities

- **George Clooney:** The epitome of Taurus charm and charisma.
- **Queen Elizabeth II:** A symbol of Taurus resilience and dedication.
- **Adele:** Her soulful voice and down-to-earth nature showcase the typical Taurus blend of talent and authenticity.

With their love for stability and comfort, Taurus brings a grounding energy to the zodiac. Their practicality and loyalty are the glue in relationships and teams, making them invaluable in personal and professional realms.

Chapter 5
GEMINI

Being a Gemini means mastering the art of conversation-and forgetting what the conversation was about.

Get ready to enter the world of Gemini, the zodiac's social butterfly and intellectual powerhouse. In this chapter, we're diving into the essence of Gemini, the sign symbolized by the Twins. Known for their dual nature, quick wit, and insatiable curiosity, Geminis bring a whirlwind of energy and intellect to every room they enter. If you're a Gemini, prepare to meet yourself in these pages. And if you're not, you're about to understand the Geminis in your life on a whole new level. From their love for conversation to their agile minds, we'll explore what makes these air signs the fascinating, multifaceted characters of the zodiac.

Zodiac Birth Dates

May 21 - June 20: The period when the sun dances into the sign of Gemini, ushering in a time of communication, curiosity, and adaptability.

Core Attributes

- **Ruling Planet:** Mercury, the gods' messenger, influences Gemini's exceptional communication skills.
- **Element:** Air, which lends Gemini their intellectual, communicative, and flexible nature.
- **Symbol-The Twins:** Representing Gemini's dual nature and ability to see and understand multiple perspectives.

Gemini, symbolized by the Twins, signifies duality, communication, and intellectual agility. Born under the influence of Mercury, the messenger planet Gemini is gifted in the art of expression, whether it's through speaking, writing, or other creative forms. This Mercurial influence also endows them with a quick-thinking and adaptable mind, always ready to learn and explore new ideas.

As an Air sign, Geminis are often found floating in a world of concepts and abstract thoughts. They thrive in environments stimulating their intellect and allowing them to exchange ideas. This element highlights their personality, manifesting as a breezy, flexible approach to life. Geminis are the zodiac's communicators, adept at conveying their thoughts and quickly grasping others' perspectives.

Their symbol, the Twins, perfectly encapsulates the essence of Gemini. It speaks to their dual nature, an innate ability to see and understand both sides of every situation. This duality can make them wonderfully versatile and open-minded. Still, it can also lead to indecision as they try to reconcile the two sides within themselves.

Geminis are naturally curious, with a youthful energy that keeps them on a constant quest for knowledge and new experiences. They're the social butterflies of the zodiac, moving from one group to another, sparking conversations, and making connections wherever they go.

The critical characteristics of Gemini – their Mercurial intellect, airy adaptability, and dual nature – make them fascinating and dynamic individuals, always ready to engage and explore the world around them.

Personality Traits

- **Eloquence and Wit:** Geminis are known for their sharp minds and quick wit, making them excellent conversationalists and storytellers.
- **Curiosity:** They have an insatiable desire to learn and explore, often possessing various interests.

- **Adaptability:** Gemini can quickly adapt to different situations and people, making them versatile and open-minded.

Geminis are the zodiac's sparkling conversationalists and curious thinkers. Thanks to their ruling planet Mercury, their personality is marked by a vibrant blend of intellect, curiosity, and adaptability. This makes them some of the most engaging and versatile characters you'll meet.

One of Gemini's most notable traits is their eloquence. They have a way with words, whether they're chatting up a storm at a party or crafting a beautifully written piece. Their communication skills are second to none, making them excellent storytellers, writers, and speakers. With a Gemini, the conversation is never dull; it's filled with quick-witted humor and insightful observations.

Then there's their insatiable curiosity. Geminis have a thirst for knowledge that never seems to be quenched. They are interested in various subjects and love to keep themselves informed. This trait makes them lifelong learners, always up for exploring new ideas, places, and cultures.

However, their adaptability is perhaps their most defining trait. Geminis are incredibly flexible and can adjust to almost any situation. This adaptability makes them open-minded and willing to consider different perspectives. But it can also mean they're a bit unpredictable – you never quite know which side of their dual nature you will get.

But it's not all smooth sailing. Gemini's love for variety can sometimes come off as being fickle or indecisive. They can find it hard to stick to one path in their personal and professional lives. Also, their mind moves so quickly that they can sometimes be scattered or unfocused.

The Gemini personality is a delightful mix of quick intellect, endless curiosity, and the ability to adapt to any situation. They bring fresh air to any setting, but their dual nature can sometimes be a puzzle, even to themselves.

Innate Strengths

- **Communication Skills:** Whether through speaking, writing, or other forms of communication, Geminis excel in expressing themselves.
- **Intellectual Agility:** Their ability to think quickly and learn fast makes them natural problem-solvers.
- **Social Skills:** Gemini's charm and charisma make them popular in social circles and able to engage with various people.

With their versatile and dynamic nature, Geminis possess a range of strengths that make them stand out in any crowd. At the heart of their strengths lies their exceptional communication skills. Thanks to their ruling planet, Mercury, Geminis have a natural flair for speaking, writing, and expressing ideas. They can articulate their thoughts with clarity and charm, making them effective communicators in personal and professional settings.

Another significant strength of Gemini is its intellectual agility. They have quick minds, capable of absorbing, processing, and reacting to information at an impressive pace. This makes them fast learners and adept at adapting to new ideas and concepts. Whether picking up a new language, mastering a new technology, or simply staying on top of current events, Geminis are always a few steps ahead.

Socially, Geminis shine bright. Their friendly and charismatic nature makes them popular in any social setting. They can effortlessly mingle and converse with different groups, quickly making connections and friendships. This social prowess also allows them to build extensive networks in their personal and professional lives.

Curiosity is another key strength. Geminis are naturally curious and always eager to explore and understand the world around them. This curiosity drives them to new experiences and learnings, keeping their lives dynamic and exciting. It also makes them open to different perspectives, enhancing their ability to relate to various people and situations.

Lastly, Geminis' adaptability is a powerful asset. Their ability to adapt, evolve, and embrace new circumstances is invaluable in a constantly changing world. They're not afraid of change; they often thrive in it, making them well-suited to environments that require flexibility and innovation.

In summary, the strengths of Gemini – outstanding communication, intellectual agility, social skills, curiosity, and adaptability – make them versatile and engaging individuals, capable of navigating a gambit of situations with ease and charisma.

Challenges to Overcome

- **Inconsistency:** Their dual nature can sometimes lead to a conflict of consistency in thoughts and actions.
- **Indecisiveness:** With so many interests and ideas, Geminis can struggle to make decisions or stick to one path.
- **Surface-level Interests:** Sometimes, their curiosity can be fleeting, leading them to skim the surface of subjects without delving deeper.

While Geminis possess many strengths, they also have their share of weaknesses that can pose challenges in their lives. One notable area for improvement is their tendency to be consistent. Geminis are known for their dual nature, which can sometimes translate into a lack of consistency in their actions and thoughts. This can make them seem unreliable or flaky, as they might change their minds frequently or need help to stick to commitments.

Another area where Geminis might find themselves struggling is indecisiveness. With their minds always racing with different thoughts and ideas, making a definitive decision can be daunting. This indecisiveness isn't just about choosing a restaurant for dinner; it extends to significant life choices, where their ability to see all sides of a situation can lead to paralysis by analysis.

Geminis also have a penchant for surface-level interests. Their curiosity is vast, but it can be fleeting. They might find themselves enthusiastically diving into a new hobby or project, only to lose interest quickly and move on to the next shiny thing. This trait can hinder them from developing deep expertise or lasting passions in certain areas.

Additionally, their adaptability and flexibility, while generally strengths, can sometimes manifest as a lack of direction. They're so adaptable that they might find it challenging to determine what they truly want and stand firm in their pursuits.

Lastly, Geminis is a bit superficial in their relationships. Their love for variety and excitement can sometimes come at the expense of depth and stability in their connections. They might find it challenging to delve into a relationship's more profound, more emotional aspects, preferring to keep things light and breezy.

Gemini's challenges – inconsistency, indecisiveness, surface-level interests, lack of direction, and a tendency towards superficiality –

are reflections of their versatile and dynamic nature. Recognizing and addressing these weaknesses can help Geminis find more stability and depth in their pursuits and relationships.

Relational Dynamics in Love and Friendship

- **Ideal Partners:** Those who match Gemini's intellectual energy and respect their need for variety and stimulation.
- **Friendship Dynamics:** Gemini seeks intellectually stimulating friends and is open to spontaneous adventures.

Gemini, known for their intellectual curiosity and social agility, approach relationships with a blend of wit, communication, and a desire for variety. In love and friendship, they seek connections that resonate with their dynamic nature and stimulate their ever-active minds.

In romantic relationships, Gemini is captivating and playful. They are drawn to partners who can equal their intellectual curiosity and share their love for conversation and exploration. A Gemini in love is communicative, lively, and enjoys a relationship filled with mental stimulation and social activity. They pair well with signs that appreciate their versatility and can offer the intellectual engagement they crave.

When it comes to friendships, Gemini is the quintessential social butterfly. They enjoy a wide circle of friends from various backgrounds, offering different perspectives and experiences. Their friends value Gemini's adaptability, ability to liven up any conversation, and readiness to try new things. Gemini thrives in intellectually stimulating and spontaneous friendships, allowing them the freedom to be their multifaceted selves.

Most Compatible Signs with Gemini:

Libra: Air sign Libra complements Gemini's communicative nature with a harmonious and balanced approach. This pairing is booming due to their shared love for intellectual discussions, social gatherings, and a mutual appreciation for the arts. Together, they form a relationship that is intellectually enriching and socially engaging.

Aquarius: Aquarius brings a unique and innovative dynamic to Gemini's life. This pairing thrives on intellectual stimulation and a shared desire for social change and exploration. Aquarius' visionary nature and Gemini's adaptability create an exciting and mentally stimulating relationship.

Aries: Fire sign Aries offers a passionate and energetic match for Gemini's lively spirit. This relationship is successful because of Aries' enthusiasm and Gemini's intellectual agility, creating a dynamic and adventurous partnership. They enjoy a relationship filled with action, lively debates, and new experiences.

Sagittarius: Sagittarius and Gemini share an intellectual and physical love for exploration. This pairing is booming due to their mutual desire for adventure, learning, and understanding different cultures and philosophies. Their relationship is marked by growth, laughter, and a shared journey of discovery.

Gemini finds fulfilling relationships with signs that share their love for intellectual stimulation, social interaction, and a sense of adventure. Their ideal partnerships balance their need for variety with a sense of understanding and intellectual companionship.

Gemini's approach to love and friendships is as dynamic and multifaceted as their personality. Their innate charm and communication skills make them attractive partners and friends. Still, their dual nature can add complexity to these relationships.

In romantic relationships, Gemini values intellectual stimulation and variety. They are attracted to partners who can engage in stimulating conversations and share their sense of curiosity. A mental connection is often just as important as a physical or emotional one for a Gemini. Air signs like Libra and Aquarius can be great matches, as they share Gemini's love for intellectual engagement and social interaction. Fire signs like Aries and Leo can also complement Gemini's energy, offering the excitement and dynamism that Geminis enjoy.

However, Gemini's need for variety and stimulation can sometimes lead to relationship instability. They may find it challenging to settle down or commit to one person if they feel it might limit their freedom or intellectual growth. Their partner's understanding and willingness to keep the relationship fresh and engaging are crucial.

In friendships, Gemini is the life of the party. They are friendly, fun, and always up for an adventure. They make friends quickly and have a wide social circle. However, their tendency to flit from one group to another can sometimes be perceived as superficial. Building more profound, long-lasting friendships requires Gemini to balance their love for variety with a commitment to nurturing their friendships.

Geminis are most compatible with friends who are flexible and open-minded. They enjoy the company of those willing to explore new ideas and try new activities and who can keep up with their fast-paced lifestyle. Maintaining friendships with more grounded signs, like Taurus or Capricorn, can benefit Geminis, providing some much-needed stability and depth.

Overall, Gemini's strengths lie in love and friendships: adaptability, intellectual curiosity, and communication skills. To form lasting and meaningful relationships, they must balance their passion for diversity and excitement with a commitment to deeper connections.

Career Insights

- **Career Paths:** Fields that require intellectual engagement, communication, and adaptability are ideal for Gemini.
- **In the Workplace:** Gemini's versatility and ability to juggle multiple tasks make them valuable team members.
- **Career Tips:** Embracing depth and focus can enhance Gemini's career prospects and personal growth.

Gemini, characterized by their intellectual curiosity and communicative prowess, brings a dynamic and versatile approach to their professional life. In their career, Gemini values diversity, mental stimulation, and opportunities to leverage their strong communication skills. Their approach to work is often marked by adaptability, ingenuity, and a preference for tasks that engage their mental faculties.

One of Gemini's greatest strengths in their career is their exceptional communication abilities. Whether verbal or written, Gemini excels in articulating ideas and information effectively, making them excellent in teaching, public speaking, or writing roles. Their knack for clear and persuasive communication is a significant asset in any field that requires understandably conveying complex information.

Their versatility and adaptability are other key strengths. Gemini can quickly adjust to new situations and tasks, making them effective in dynamic work environments with constant change. This adaptability and their natural curiosity allow them to learn new skills and information rapidly, keeping them ahead in fast-paced industries.

However, Gemini may sometimes struggle with focus and consistency. Their interest in a wide range of topics can lead to a scattered approach to work, and they might find it challenging to stick with one project for an extended period. Balancing their love for variety with the need to complete tasks is crucial for their professional success.

Most Suitable Work/Career Choices for Gemini:

Journalism and Writing: Gemini's strong communication skills and curiosity make them well-suited for careers in journalism and writing. Their ability to gather, process, and present information engagingly is an asset in these fields.

Teaching and Education: Gemini's love for sharing knowledge and interacting with others aligns well with a career in teaching or education. Their ability to explain complex concepts makes them effective educators.

Marketing and Public Relations: The dynamic marketing and public relations field suits Gemini's adaptable and communicative nature. Their creativity and understanding of different perspectives are valuable in crafting compelling marketing and PR strategies.

Technology and IT: The ever-evolving tech industry offers the mental stimulation and variety that Gemini craves. Their quick learning ability and adaptability make them suitable for technology and information systems roles.

Event Planning and Coordination: Gemini's organizational skills and ability to multitask make them effective in event planning and coordination. Their knack for handling various aspects of an event and communicating effectively with stakeholders is crucial in this field.

Gemini excels in work environments that offer variety, intellectual challenges, and opportunities to utilize their communication skills. They are most successful in careers that allow them to engage in diverse tasks, learn continuously, and interact with various people.

Famous Gemini Personalities

- **Angelina Jolie:** A testament to Gemini's charisma and versatility.
- **Kanye West:** Showcasing Gemini's creativity and ever-changing nature.
- **Johnny Depp:** A reflection of Gemini's adaptability and diverse talents.

For Gemini, versatility and communication are their hallmarks in the zodiac. With their quick wit and adaptable nature, Geminis bring a dynamic energy to interactions and environments, thriving in social connections and intellectual pursuits in both personal and professional settings.

Chapter 6
CANCER

Cancer means having a heart as deep as the ocean and emotions that sometimes tidal wave.

Now, let's delve into Cancer, the zodiac's nurturing heart. In this chapter, we explore the depths of Cancer, a sign marked by emotional depth, intuition, and a strong sense of home and family. Cancers are the zodiac's caretakers, known for their compassionate and protective nature. If you're a Cancer, this chapter will feel like coming home. If you're not, you're about to understand the Cancers in your life with newfound appreciation. From their powerful emotional intelligence to their unwavering loyalty, we'll uncover the layers that make this Water sign an emotional core of the zodiac.

Zodiac Birth Dates

June 21 - July 22: The time when the sun enters Cancer, marking a period of emotional depth, introspection, and nurturing.

Core Attributes

- **Ruling Planet:** The Moon, governing emotions and intuition, strongly influences Cancer's personality.
- **Element:** Water, which speaks to Cancer's fluid, emotional, and intuitive nature.
- **Symbol-The Crab:** Representing Cancer's ability to navigate emotional and material realms and their protective shell.

Cancer, symbolized by the Crab, is deeply rooted in the emotional and intuitive realms. Governed by the Moon, Cancers are in tune with the ebb and flow of emotions, both their own and those of others. This lunar influence imparts a remarkable sensitivity and a solid connection to their inner world, shaping much of their personality and approach to life.

As a Water sign, Cancer embodies the fluidity and depth of this element. They are adept at navigating the emotional waters, often possessing a profound empathetic understanding that allows them to connect with others deeply. This emotional depth is a source of strength and vulnerability, as it enables them to empathize and makes them susceptible to being deeply affected by the emotions around them.

The Crab symbol is particularly fitting for Cancer. It represents their ability to exist in emotional and practical realms and their protective nature. Like a crab in its shell, Cancer can be protective of themselves and their loved ones, often creating a safe, nurturing space for those they care about. The shell also signifies their tendency to retreat and protect themselves when they feel threatened or vulnerable.

Cancers are often driven by their need for security and stability, especially in their personal lives. They cherish home and family, and their actions and decisions are geared toward building and maintaining a harmonious and secure home environment.

In summary, the key characteristics of Cancer – their lunar-driven emotions, water-like depth and fluidity, and the protective nature symbolized by the Crab – create a personality that is nurturing, intuitive, and deeply connected to the emotional world.

Personality Traits

- **Empathy and Sensitivity:** Cancers are highly empathetic, often able to sense the emotions and needs of others.

- **Nurturing Nature:** They are natural caregivers, always ready to offer support and comfort.
- **Intuitive:** Cancer individuals often rely on intuition, picking up on subtle cues and underlying emotional currents.

Cancers, with their deep emotional resonance and intuitive nature, exhibit a rich tapestry of personality traits that are both endearing and complex. At the heart of a Cancer's personality is unparalleled empathy. They possess an instinctive ability to understand and share the feelings of others. This talent makes Cancers exceptional listeners and compassionate companions. This empathetic nature often makes them the confidants in their social circles, where friends and family seek their understanding and support.

Their nurturing disposition is another defining trait. Cancers have a natural instinct to protect and care for those around them. They often take on the role of caretakers, personally or professionally, offering a shoulder to lean on and a listening ear. This nurturing quality extends to their love of home and family, central to their lives. Creating a comfortable and secure home environment is often a top priority for a Cancer.

Intuition is a crucial aspect of Cancer's personality. Guided by their ruling planet, the Moon, they are in tune with their instincts. This intuitive sense allows them to pick up on subtleties in their environment and the people around them, often sensing things others might miss. It's common for Cancer to make decisions based on their gut feelings, which often turn out to be correct.

However, Cancer's sensitivity can also be a double-edged sword. They can be easily hurt or affected by harsh words or hostile environments. This sensitivity often leads them to build a protective shell around themselves, much like their crab symbol, to guard against potential emotional hurt.

Lastly, Cancers are known for their moodiness. Influenced by the ever-changing Moon, their emotions can be fluid, leading to periods of introspection or melancholy. Understanding and navigating these emotional tides is a significant part of a Cancer's life journey.

In essence, Cancer's personality traits – empathy, nurturing nature, intuition, sensitivity, and moodiness – paint a picture of an individual deeply connected to the emotional realm, caring deeply for others, and guided by their inner feelings.

Innate Strengths

- **Emotional Intelligence:** Cancers keenly understand their own and others' emotions, making them compassionate friends and partners.
- **Loyalty:** Once you have a Cancer's loyalty, it's unwavering. Commitment to their loved ones is innate.
- **Creativity:** Their rich emotional inner world often leads to a strong creative streak, whether in art, writing, or other forms of expression.

Cancers possess a range of strengths that stem from their deep emotional intelligence and caring nature. One of their most notable strengths is their emotional intelligence. Cancers have an innate ability to understand and process emotions, both their own and those of others. This emotional understanding allows them to navigate complex interpersonal dynamics with compassion and empathy, making them valued friends, partners, and colleagues.

Another significant strength is their loyalty. Once you have earned the trust and affection of a Cancer, they are steadfastly loyal. Trough thick and thin, Cancer stands by its loved ones, offering unwavering support and protection. This loyalty also makes them incredibly reliable; they are all in when a Cancer commits to something.

Cancer's nurturing nature is also a key strength. They are naturally inclined to care for others, creating a sense of warmth and security for those in their inner circle. This extends beyond personal relationships; in the workplace, Cancers often become the unofficial caretakers, ensuring everyone is heard and cared for.

Their creativity is another area where Cancers shine. Influenced by their rich inner world and emotional depth, many Cancers find expression in creative pursuits. Whether it's art, music, writing, or culinary arts, Cancers can infuse emotion and meaning into their creations.

Cancers are incredibly intuitive. Intuitively, they often rely on their gut feelings when making decisions, often to the correct outcome. This intuition, coupled with their ability to read situations and people, can be a powerful tool in their personal and professional lives.

Cancer's strengths – emotional intelligence, loyalty, nurturing nature, creativity, and intuition – make them compassionate and caring individuals, deeply in tune with the world around them and the people they care about.

Challenges to Overcome

- **Over-Sensitivity:** Their deep sensitivity can sometimes lead to being easily hurt or offended.

- **Moodiness:** The influence of the Moon can lead to fluctuating moods, making Cancers sometimes seem unpredictable.
- **Tendency to Cling:** Their need for security and fear of abandonment can make them clingy or overly dependent in relationships.

Despite their many strengths, Cancers also face specific weaknesses that stem from their profoundly emotional nature. One of the most prominent is their tendency to be overly sensitive. Cancers can take things to heart and may get easily hurt by comments or actions that others might brush off. This sensitivity, while part of their empathetic charm, can sometimes lead them to feel overwhelmed by emotional stress or become overly defensive.

Another weakness is their moodiness. Being ruled by the Moon, Cancers are subject to emotional fluctuations that can be confusing not only to those around them but also to themselves. Their moods can change rapidly, and they might struggle to maintain dynamic consistency. This can make them seem unpredictable or difficult to understand at times.

Cancers also have a propensity to cling to the past. They often find comfort in nostalgia, but this can turn into a reluctance to let go of old hurts or grudges. Holding onto negative experiences can hinder their emotional growth and affect their current relationships.

Additionally, Cancers can be prone to possessiveness, especially in close relationships. Their deep fear of losing loved ones can manifest in overly protective or controlling behaviors. While this stems from a place of love and care, it can be smothering for those on the receiving end.

Lastly, their need for security and fear of rejection can sometimes lead Cancers to avoid risk taking or stepping out of their comfort zone. They might prefer to stay in the safety of familiar environments and relationships, which can limit their opportunities for growth and new experiences.

Cancer's challenges – over-sensitivity, moodiness, clinging to the past, possessiveness, and a reluctance to take risks – are closely linked to their emotional depth. Recognizing and managing these aspects can help Cancers find a healthier balance and foster more fulfilling relationships and life experiences.

Relationship Dynamics in Love and Friendship

- **Ideal Partners:** Those who understand and respect Cancer's emotional depth and need for security. Earth signs like Taurus and Virgo can offer stability. In contrast, Water signs like Scorpio and Pisces resonate with their expressive nature.
- **Friendship Dynamics:** Cancers value deep, meaningful friendships. They need friends who are understanding, patient, and willing to explore emotional depths.

With their deep emotional sensitivity and nurturing spirit, Cancer approaches relationships with an emphasis on care, emotional depth, and a strong sense of home and family. They seek connections that offer warmth, security, and mutual understanding in love and friendship.

In romantic relationships, Cancer is the epitome of caring and devotion. They are drawn to partners who value emotional connection and who appreciate the depth of Cancer's feelings. A Cancer in love is protective, loyal, and deeply intuitive about their partner's needs. They thrive in relationships where emotional security is a priority and where they can express their caring nature fully.

Friendships for Cancer are often longstanding and based on a foundation of trust and emotional support. They are the friends who will be there unwaveringly, offering a listening ear and a comforting presence. Cancer values heartfelt and nurturing friendships where they can share their innermost feelings and experiences.

Most Compatible Signs with Cancer:

Pisces: Fellow Water sign Pisces complements Cancer's emotional depth with its intuitive and empathetic nature. This pairing is successful due to their mutual understanding of each other's emotional needs and a shared love for creativity and romance. Together, they create a profoundly moving and spiritually enriching bond.

Scorpio: Scorpio brings intensity and passion to the relationship, resonating well with Cancer's need for emotional intimacy and security. This pairing is successful because of their shared depth of feeling and a mutual desire for a committed and transformative relationship.

Taurus: Earth sign Taurus offers the stability and practicality that Cancer admires. This relationship is successful because Taurus provides security and reliability, while Cancer brings warmth and emotional depth. Together, they form a nurturing and harmonious bond.

Virgo: Virgo's practical and attentive nature complements Cancer's emotional and caring approach. This pairing is successful due to Virgo's ability to provide reasonable support and Cancer's knack for emotional understanding, creating a balanced and supportive relationship.

Cancer finds the most fulfilling relationships with signs that offer emotional depth, understanding, and a sense of security. Their ideal partnerships provide a strong emotional connection, mutual care, and a shared value for home and family.

Career Insights

- **Career Paths:** Cancers excel in careers that allow them to care for and support others, like healthcare, social work, or education.
- **In the Workplace:** They are cooperative and empathetic colleagues, often the emotional anchor of their team.
- **Career Tips:** Embracing their emotional intelligence and creativity can lead to fulfilling career paths. It is crucial to balance their need for security with the courage to step out of their comfort zone.

Cancer, known for its depth of feeling and nurturing instincts, brings a compassionate and intuitive approach to its professional life. In their career, Cancer values emotional connections, a supportive work environment, and opportunities to utilize their caring and empathetic nature. Their approach to work is often characterized by a strong sense of loyalty, a dedication to the well-being of others, and a preference for stability and security.

One of Cancer's greatest strengths in their career is their empathetic and nurturing disposition. This makes them particularly effective in roles that involve caring for others, whether in healthcare, education, or customer service. Their ability to understand and respond to the emotional needs of others makes them invaluable in careers that benefit from a high degree of emotional intelligence.

Their loyalty and dedication are other key strengths. Cancer is often deeply committed to their work and colleagues, creating camaraderie and trust. This loyalty and their desire for stability make them reliable and consistent performers in their chosen fields.

However, Cancer may sometimes struggle with handling criticism or stressful situations. Their emotional sensitivity can lead to taking feedback too personally or feeling overwhelmed in high-pressure environments. Finding ways to manage their emotional responses and seeking supportive work environments is crucial for their professional well-being.

Most Suitable Work/Career Choices for Cancer:

Healthcare and Nursing: Cancer's caring nature and desire to help others make them well-suited for healthcare, nursing, or caregiving careers. Their empathy and compassion are essential in these roles, where patient care and emotional support are paramount.

Education and Childcare: Cancer's nurturing instincts and ability to connect with people make them excellent teachers, childcare providers, or counselors. Their capacity to create safe and supportive learning environments helps them excel in educational settings.

Human Resources: The field of human resources suits Cancer's people-oriented approach. Their empathy and understanding of human dynamics make them effective in roles that involve employee relations, support, and development.

Social Work and Counseling: Cancer's inclination to help and support others is a natural fit for social work or counseling. Their ability to empathize and provide emotional support is valuable in assisting individuals to navigate personal challenges.

Creative Arts: Cancer's rich inner world and emotional depth can find expression in the creative arts. Whether in writing, music, or visual arts, Cancer can channel their emotions into creative endeavors, making impactful and meaningful art.

In summary, Cancer excels in work environments that value emotional connections, offer stability, and allow them to care for and support others. They are most successful in careers that leverage their empathetic nature, nurturing instincts, and dedication to the well-being of others.

Famous Cancer Personalities

- **Meryl Streep:** A shining example of Cancer's emotional depth and artistic talent.
- **Tom Hanks:** Reflecting Cancer's warmth, sensitivity, and versatility.
- **Selena Gomez:** Showcases Cancer's nurturing spirit and emotional expressiveness.

For Cancer, sensitivity and nurturing define their essence in the zodiac. Their profound emotional intelligence and caring nature make them the heart of relationships and groups, providing support and compassion in both personal and professional spheres.

Chapter 7
LEO

Being a Leo means mastering the art of being unforgettable, one grand entrance at a time.

S tep into the radiant world of Leo, the zodiac's natural-born leader and showstopper. In this chapter, we celebrate the essence of Leo, symbolized by the majestic lion. Known for their dramatic flair, unwavering confidence, and big-hearted generosity, Leos embodies strength and charisma. You'll recognize your regal nature in these pages if you're a Leo. And if you're not, you'll gain a deeper appreciation for Leo's bold approach to life. From their love for the spotlight to their warm, protective nature, we'll delve into what makes these fire signs the vibrant rulers of the zodiac.

Zodiac Birth Dates

July 23 - August 22: The time when the Sun reigns in Leo, bringing forth a period of boldness, creativity, and warmth.

Core Attributes

- **Ruling Planet:** The Sun, which bestows Leo vitality, creativity, and a desire to shine.
- **Element:** Fire, fueling their dynamic energy, passion, and charismatic presence.
- **Symbol- The Lion:** Symbolizing Leo's regal demeanor, courage, and protective nature.

Leo, symbolized by the regal lion, is characterized by an air of royalty and a fiery spirit. Ruled by the Sun, Leos possess a natural radiance and vitality that draws others to them. The Sun's influence endows them with a strong sense of self, creativity, and a desire to be in the spotlight. They embody their ruling celestial body's warmth, brightness, and life-giving qualities.

As a Fire sign, Leo is dynamic, passionate, and energetic. This element fuels their charismatic presence and their zest for life. Leos are often seen as the life of the party, bringing warmth, light, and excitement wherever they go. Their fiery nature also contributes to their courageous and bold approach to life, not shying away from challenges or opportunities to showcase their talents.

The symbol of the lion perfectly captures Leo's essence – they are confident, proud, and often have a regal bearing. Like the king of the jungle, Leos are natural leaders, exuding authority and a protective spirit over those they care about. They are courageous and not afraid to take risks, often inspiring others with their bravery.

Leo's desire for recognition and admiration is also a key characteristic. They thrive on appreciation and applause, and this need for validation is often at the core of their actions. They want to be seen, heard and admired for their unique abilities and contributions.

The key characteristics of Leo – their Sun-ruled radiance, fiery energy, regal nature, and desire for recognition – combine to create a personality that is bold, bright, and unapologetically vibrant.

Personality Traits

- **Confident and Charismatic:** Leos are natural leaders with an air of confidence that others find magnetic.
- **Generous and Warm-Hearted:** They have big hearts and often give help and support to others.
- **Creative and Expressive:** Leos are drawn to artistic pursuits where they can express themselves and bask in

the admiration of others.

With their sun-ruled charisma, Leos exhibit personality traits that make them both inspiring and captivating. One of the most defining traits of a Leo is their confidence. They carry themselves with an air of assurance and pride, often exuding a natural authority. This confidence isn't just for show; it's a genuine belief in their abilities and worth, making them natural leaders and trendsetters.

Alongside their confidence, Leos are known for their generous and warm-hearted nature. They have big hearts and often go out of their way to help, support, and cheer up those around them. This generosity isn't limited to material things; they're also generous with their time, attention, and affection, making them great friends and companions.

Creativity and a love for expression are also central to Leo's personality. Whether through art, fashion, speech, or writing, Leo has a natural flair for creativity. They enjoy expressing themselves and often seek platforms to share their talents and ideas with others.

However, Leo's personality isn't all about being bold and center-stage. They have a playful and humorous side, often bringing laughter and joy to those around them. They enjoy the lighter side of life and can be incredibly charming and fun to be around.

Yet, for all their outward confidence, Leos can be surprisingly sensitive. They care deeply about how they are perceived and can be hurt by criticism or neglect. This sensitivity often lies hidden behind their confident exterior, only seen by those who know them well.

In essence, Leo's personality traits – confidence, generosity, creativity, playfulness, and hidden sensitivity – create a complex and charismatic individual who is both a leader and a giver, an artist and a protector.

Innate Strengths

- **Leadership Abilities:** Leos are born leaders, able to inspire and motivate those around them with their vision and enthusiasm.
- **Loyalty:** Once committed, Leos are fiercely loyal and protective of their loved ones and causes.
- **Resilience:** Leo possesses a strong spirit and an ability to bounce back from challenging situations.

Leos possess a constellation of strengths that shine brightly in their personal and professional lives. At the heart of these strengths is their natural leadership ability. Born under the Sun's radiant influence, Leos inspire and motivate those around them with confidence and charisma. They have a unique way of making others feel seen and valued, which endears them to many. Whether in a leadership position or part of a team, their presence is often a guiding light that others are drawn to.

Another significant strength of Leo is their loyalty. When Leos care about someone, their commitment is unwavering. They are adamantly protective of anyone they love and will go to great lengths to support and defend them. This loyalty extends beyond personal relationships to their principles and beliefs, making them steadfast and reliable in all aspects of life.

Resilience is also a defining strength of Leo. They possess a strong spirit and an innate ability to bounce back from setbacks. Their optimism and self-belief fuel their resilience, allowing them to emerge stonger iafter facing tough challenges. This resilience often inspires others, showcasing their ability to overcome obstacles with grace and determination.

Creativity is another area where Leos excel. Their sun-ruled nature gives them a vibrant imagination and a flair for the dramatic. This creativity can manifest in various ways – from artistic endeavors to innovative problem-solving. Leos often find joy and fulfillment in expressing their creative side, professionally or as a hobby.

Lastly, Leos have a generous spirit. They are not only generous with material things but also with their time, attention, and affection. This generosity makes them beloved friends, family members, and colleagues, as they are always ready to lend a helping hand or offer a listening ear.

Leo's strengths – leadership, loyalty, resilience, creativity, and generosity – make them dynamic and influential individuals, capable of leading the charge and nurturing those around them.

Challenges to Overcome

- **Pride and Ego:** Their strong sense of pride can sometimes lead to arrogance or a refusal to show vulnerability.
- **Sensitivity to Criticism:** Despite their bold front, Leos can be sensitive to criticism, taking it more personally than intended.
- **Tendency to Dominate:** Their natural leadership can sometimes become a desire to control or dominate situations.

Despite their many strengths, Leos also face specific weaknesses that stem from their bold and energetic nature. One notable weakness is their pride and sometimes oversized ego. Leos have a strong sense of self-worth, which, while generally positive, can tip into arrogance. They might struggle to admit mistakes or show vulnerability, as doing so feels like a blow to their pride. This can lead to challenges in personal and professional relationships, where humility and openness are necessary.

Another area where Leos might need help is in their sensitivity to criticism. Despite their confident exterior, they can take criticism to heart, often feeling deeply wounded by negative feedback or perceived slights. This sensitivity, hidden beneath a bold façade, can affect their decision-making and willingness to take risks, especially if they fear judgment or failure.

Leos can also exhibit a tendency to dominate. Their natural leadership skills and desire to be in the spotlight can sometimes become a need for control. They might unintentionally overshadow others or assert their opinions too forcefully, which can be off-putting or lead to conflict, particularly in team dynamics.

Additionally, their desire for recognition and admiration can sometimes become a weakness. Leos thrive on validation and can become disheartened or frustrated if their efforts go unnoticed. This need for constant appreciation can lead to a dependency on external validation rather than finding satisfaction from within.

Leo's love for extravagance can sometimes lead to indulgence. They enjoy living life to the fullest, which is generally positive but can sometimes result in over-the-top behavior or spending, mainly if they equate material success or luxury with self-worth.

Leo's weaknesses – pride and ego, sensitivity to criticism, a tendency to dominate, a need for recognition, and a penchant for extravagance – reflect their sunny and commanding nature. Recognizing and balancing these aspects can help Leos maintain harmonious relationships and lead more fulfilling lives.

Relationship Dynamics in Love and Friendship

- **Ideal Partners:** Those who can match Leo's passion and zest for life while respecting their need for independence and admiration.
- **Friendship Dynamics:** Leos seek loyal, entertaining friends who appreciate their generous nature and love for the spotlight.

Leo, known for their vibrant charisma and generous heart, approaches relationships with a blend of warmth, loyalty, and a flair for the dramatic. In love and friendship, they seek connections that resonate with their bold spirit and appreciate their need for appreciation and respect.

In romantic relationships, Leo is passionate and wholeheartedly devoted. They thrive with partners who match their enthusiasm and energy and offer the admiration and loyalty Leo craves. A Leo in love is a generous, affectionate partner, often going out of their way to make their significant other feel valued and special. They are naturally drawn to partners who are confident, independent, and equally expressive in their affection.

Regarding friendships, Leo is the life of the party – a loyal, fun-loving, and generous friend. They gravitate towards friendships that are lively, honest, and full of mutual admiration. Their friends value Leo's warm-hearted nature and ability to bring excitement and joy to their gatherings.

Most Compatible Signs with Leo:

Aries: Fire sign Aries provides a dynamic and energetic match for Leo's exuberant nature. This pairing is successful due to their mutual enthusiasm for life and a shared desire for adventure and excitement. Aries and Leo admire each other's strength and confidence, creating a passionate and respectful relationship.

Sagittarius: Sagittarius complements Leo's love for the dramatic with their sense of adventure and optimism. This relationship thrives on both signs' love for exploration, fun, and a shared sense of humor. Together, they enjoy a vibrant, adventurous, and joyous partnership.

Gemini: Air sign Gemini brings intellectual stimulation and a sense of playfulness to Leo's life. This pairing is successful because Gemini's communicative and social nature meshes well with Leo's love for social engagement and attention. Together, they create a relationship that is both intellectually stimulating and entertaining.

Libra: Libra offers a harmonious balance to Leo's dynamic nature. This relationship is successful due to Libra's ability to appreciate Leo's need for admiration and their shared love for the finer things in life. Together, they enjoy a partnership that is both romantic and aesthetically pleasing.

Leo finds fulfilling relationships with signs that share their zest for life, offer intellectual and social stimulation, and provide the admiration and loyalty they cherish. Their ideal partnerships balance their bold nature with mutual respect and admiration.

Career Insights

- **Career Paths:** Roles that allow Leos to lead, create, and be in the spotlight are ideal, such as management, entertainment, or any creative field.

- **In the Workplace:** They are motivating and charismatic colleagues but may need to balance their desire for recognition with collaboration.
- **Career Tips:** Embracing humility and teamwork can enhance Leo's career growth and personal development.

With their natural flair for drama and leadership, Leo brings a commanding presence to their professional life. Leo seeks opportunities to shine, lead, and express their creativity in their career. Their approach to work is characterized by ambition, a desire for recognition, and an innate ability to inspire others.

One of Leo's greatest strengths in their career is their charismatic leadership. They possess the confidence and vitality to take charge and motivate their teams, making them excellent leaders, managers, and directors. Their ability to engage and rally people around a common goal is a significant asset, particularly in roles that require a figurehead or spokesperson.

Their creative talents are also a notable strength. Leo's flair for the dramatic and artistic sensibility often drives them towards the arts, entertainment, and fields that allow them to craft and share a vision. They thrive in environments that appreciate their creative input and offer a platform to showcase their work.

However, Leo may sometimes struggle with issues of ego and recognition. They strongly need to be appreciated and can become disheartened if they feel undervalued. Balancing their need for acknowledgment with a team-oriented approach can enhance their professional relationships and success.

Most Suitable Work/Career Choices for Leo:

Entertainment Industry: Leo's dramatic presence and creative talents make them natural in the entertainment industry, whether as actors, directors, or producers. Their ability to captivate an audience is key to their success in these roles.

Corporate Leadership: Leo's leadership qualities make them well-suited for executive positions in the corporate world. Their ambition and drive for success help them excel in roles that require vision and the ability to lead a company or team toward its goals.

Event Planning and Promotion: Leo's dynamic and sociable nature is perfect for a career in event planning and promotion. Their organizational skills and ability to generate excitement and engagement make them successful in orchestrating memorable events.

Creative Arts: Whether in visual arts, music, or writing, Leo's creative spark drives them to success in artistic fields. Their passion for self-expression and desire to be recognized for their artistry fuel their achievements in these careers.

Education and Training: Leos are effective educators and trainers, bringing enthusiasm and a motivational style to teaching. Their ability to engage and inspire students is beneficial in academic or professional development settings.

Leo excels in work environments that allow them to utilize their leadership abilities, creative talents, and desire for recognition. They are most successful in careers that offer a stage to shine and the opportunity to lead and inspire others.

Famous Leo Personalities

- **Jennifer Lopez:** Embodies Leo's charisma, talent, and determination.

- **Barack Obama:** Reflects Leo's leadership qualities and ability to inspire.
- **Madonna:** A testament to Leo's boldness and flair for the dramatic.

For Leo, charisma and confidence shine brightly in their zodiac role. Their natural leadership and zest for life make them inspiring figures in both personal and professional spheres, drawing others to their vibrant and creative spirit.

Share Your Stars - Leave a Review!
Burn Brighter by Helping Others

"Kindness, like a boomerang, always returns."

— Unknown

Did you know that people who do kind deeds for others often feel happier and more fulfilled? It's like having a secret superpower that makes both your day and someone else's a little brighter. And guess what? You have that superpower right in your hands, or, should I say, right at the tips of your fingers.

Imagine you have a magical telescope that can see far into the world of someone just like you but who hasn't yet discovered the fascinating universe of astrology. They're curious, eager to learn, and ready to embark on their own journey of self-discovery and cosmic exploration. They're looking up at the night sky, wishing for a guide to help them navigate the stars.

Our mission is to make the magical world of astrology easy and fun for everyone. From the fiery Aries to the grounded Taurus, everyone has a place among the stars. But to reach all the future astrologers of the world, we need your help.

If you're up for the adventure, your role is to help a fellow star-gazer by sharing your thoughts about "Astrology for Beginners: A Simple Zodiac Guide to Understand the 12 Star Signs and Unlock Self-Discovery, Personality Traits, and Compatibility."

Your review doesn't need to be as long as Leo's hair or as detailed as Virgo's planner. It just needs to come from the heart. In less than a minute, you can make a huge difference.

Here's how you can make a difference:

Just scan the QR code below to leave your review:

By sharing your experience, you're not just leaving a review; you're lighting up the path for someone else's journey of self-discovery and cosmic connection. It's a small gesture that can have a big impact, like throwing a pebble into a pond and watching the ripples spread.

If helping someone find their way among the stars makes your heart glow, welcome to the club! You're exactly the kind of cosmic companion we cherish.

I'm over the moon with excitement to guide you through the zodiac and beyond. Together, we'll uncover the mysteries of the universe and maybe learn a little more about ourselves along the way.

Thank you from the depths of the Milky Way. Now, let's get back to our adventure among the stars.

- Your guide and fellow star-traveler, Honey Barnes

PS - Remember, sharing your insights is like sending a spaceship of knowledge to someone in need. If this book has illuminated your path, consider sharing it with someone else who's looking up at the sky, searching for answers.

Chapter 8
VIRGO

I'm a Virgo, which means I have a plan, a backup plan, and a backup for the backup plan.

E mbark on a journey into Virgo, the zodiac's meticulous analyst and thoughtful helper. In this chapter, we delve into the essence of Virgo, symbolized by the maiden. Virgos are the problem-solvers and organizers of the zodiac, known for their precision, practicality, and keen eye for detail. If you're a Virgo, these pages will reflect your methodical approach to life. And if you're not, you'll better understand the Virgos around you. From their dedication to perfection to their unwavering sense of duty, we'll explore what makes these earth signs the epitome of diligence and care.

Zodiac Birth Dates

August 23 - September 22: The period when the sun transits through Virgo, marking a time of practicality, analysis, and attention to detail.

Core Attributes

- **Ruling Planet:** Mercury, enhancing Virgo's analytical mind and communicative abilities.
- **Element:** Earth, grounding them in practicality, reliability, and a no-nonsense approach to life.
- **Symbol-The Maiden:** Symbolic of Virgo's purity of purpose, meticulous nature, and a nurturing spirit.

Virgo, symbolized by the maiden, is known for its meticulousness, practicality, and analytical mind. Governed by Mercury, Virgos possess a sharp intellect and a keen attention to detail. This planetary influence enhances their ability to think critically and communicate effectively. They have a natural aptitude for dissecting complex problems and finding efficient solutions.

As an Earth sign, Virgos are grounded. They are pragmatic, reliable, and down-to-earth. This earthiness manifests in a no-nonsense approach to life; they prefer dealing with tangible facts over abstract theories. Virgos are the ones who bring order out of chaos, applying their systematic and methodical approach to both their personal and professional lives.

The symbol of the maiden represents Virgo's purity of purpose and desire for perfection. They strive for excellence in everything they do, often setting high standards for themselves and others. Pursuing perfection drives their meticulous nature, as they pay close attention to every detail, ensuring nothing is overlooked.

Virgos are also known for their nurturing spirit. While they may not be as openly affectionate as some other signs, they show their care through acts of service and practical support. They often offer help in times of need, always ready with a suitable solution or a helping hand.

The key characteristics of Virgo – their analytical mind, practicality, meticulousness, and nurturing nature – combine to create a profoundly caring and intellectually sharp personality.

Personality Traits

- **Detail-Oriented and Analytical:** Virgos have an exceptional instinct for detail and possess a logical approach to solving problems.
- **Practical and Organized:** They are known for their practicality and systematic approach to life's challenges.
- **Modest and Hardworking:** Virgos are often humble and prefer to let their work speak for itself, shying away from the spotlight.

Virgos are often distinguished by personality traits that make them the meticulous and thoughtful individuals of the zodiac. One defining characteristic is their detail-oriented nature. Virgos have an exceptional ability to notice and pay attention to the minutiae that others might overlook. This attention to detail enables them to perform tasks with high precision and thoroughness, whether in their personal life or professional endeavors.

Another prominent trait of Virgos is their practical and organized approach. They are planners and list-makers, often with a clear vision of how things should be done. Their methodical approach to life ensures that everything they engage in is handled efficiently and effectively. This practicality also means they are usually grounded and realistic, rarely caught up in impractical dreams or ideas.

Modesty is a vital aspect of Virgo's personality. Despite their many talents and abilities, Virgos tend to be humble and unassuming. They often prefer to work behind the scenes rather than seek the spotlight and usually let their accomplishments speak for themselves.

Hardworking and dedicated, Virgos do not hesitate to put in the effort required to achieve their goals. They are driven by a strong sense of duty and responsibility, often going above and beyond expectations.

However, their personality is not without its complexities. Virgos can be overly critical, both of themselves and others. Their pursuit of perfection can sometimes lead to unrealistic expectations, resulting in disappointment or frustration when things don't meet their high standards.

In social situations, Virgos can be reserved and cautious. They tend to observe and analyze before opening up, which can sometimes be misinterpreted as aloofness or detachment.

Virgo's personality traits – detail-oriented, practical, modest, hardworking, critical, and reserved – paint a picture of an individual deeply committed to excellence and efficiency yet with a caring and thoughtful side often hidden beneath a reserved exterior.

Innate Strengths

- **Diligence:** Virgos are incredibly hardworking and dedicated to their tasks, often going above and beyond.
- **Reliability:** Virgos are dependable and can be counted on to follow through on their commitments.
- **Critical Thinking:** Virgos possess strong analytical skills and can dissect complex situations and find practical solutions.

Virgos have a range of strengths stemming from their analytical minds and meticulous nature. One of their most notable strengths is their diligence. Virgos are incredibly hardworking and dedicated to their tasks. They approach their work with precision and attention to detail, often going above and beyond to ensure everything is done to the best of their ability. This makes them reliable, whether in a professional setting or in personal commitments.

Another key strength of Virgos is their analytical and critical thinking skills. Their ability to assess situations critically and think logically allows them to dissect complex problems and find effective, practical solutions. This analytical approach also makes them excellent at planning and organizing, enabling them to manage tasks and projects efficiently.

Reliability is a hallmark of Virgos. You can count on them to follow through on their promises and commitments. This reliability, combined with their practical nature, makes them trusted and valued in both personal relationships and professional collaborations.

Additionally, Virgos possess a strong sense of duty and responsibility. They take their obligations seriously and often hold themselves to high standards. This sense of responsibility drives them to fulfill their roles conscientiously and serve others in meaningful ways.

Despite their critical nature, Virgos have a nurturing side. They show their care and concern through practical means, offering help and support in tangible ways. This nurturing is often expressed in subtle, understated acts of kindness, making them caring friends, partners, and colleagues.

Virgo's strengths – diligence, analytical thinking, reliability, sense of duty, and nurturing nature – make them invaluable in any environment, known for their ability to bring order, efficiency, and a caring touch to the tasks and relationships they engage in.

Challenges to Overcome

- **Overcritical:** Their attention to detail can sometimes lead to excessive criticism of themselves and others.
- **Worry and Anxiety:** They tend to worry about things not being perfect, which can lead to stress and anxiety.
- **Reserved Nature:** Virgos may hold back in social situations, sometimes appearing aloof or overly severe.

While Virgos possess many admirable qualities, they also have weaknesses that can pose challenges. One significant weakness is their tendency to be overly critical. Virgos' attention to detail and pursuit of perfection often lead them to set very high standards, not just for themselves but for others as well. This can result in a critical attitude that sometimes comes across as nitpicking or fault-finding, potentially straining relationships and causing self-doubt.

Another area where Virgos might struggle is with worry and anxiety. Their desire for order and perfection can sometimes lead them to fret excessively about the possibility of things going wrong. This tendency to overthink and worry about the minutiae can lead to stress and hinder their ability to enjoy the present moment.

Virgos can also be reserved in nature, which can sometimes be misinterpreted as coldness or aloofness. Their cautious approach to opening up and tendency to analyze before expressing emotions can create barriers to forming close relationships. This reserved demeanor might prevent others from seeing their personality's more caring and nurturing side.

Additionally, their practical and analytical mindset, while generally a strength, can sometimes limit their ability to embrace spontaneity or appreciate life's more whimsical aspects. They may find it challenging to let go and enjoy moments that can't be planned or analyzed.

Lastly, Virgos' need for control and order can sometimes lead to reluctance to delegate or trust others to meet their standards. This can lead to taking on too much by themselves, resulting in burnout and feeling overwhelmed.

Virgo's challenges – overly critical, prone to worry, reserved, sometimes excessively practical, and reluctant to delegate – stem from their strengths. Recognizing and managing these aspects can help Virgos find a more balanced approach to life and relationships.

Relationship Dynamics in Love and Friendship

- **Ideal Partners:** Those who appreciate Virgo's practicality and support their perfectionist tendencies while offering emotional warmth.
- **Friendship Dynamics:** Virgos value friendships based on mutual respect and shared intellectual interests, often preferring a few close friends over a large social circle.

Virgo, characterized by meticulous attention to detail and a thoughtful nature, approaches relationships with practicality, loyalty, and a caring spirit. In love and friendship, they seek connections that resonate with their analytical mind and value their desire for order and stability.

In romantic relationships, Virgo is a dedicated and considerate partner. They are drawn to individuals who appreciate their practical approach to life and who can understand their often understated way of showing affection. A Virgo in love is attentive and supportive and always strives to make the relationship work more efficiently. They thrive with partners who value communication and integrity and can appreciate Virgo's often subtle expressions of love and care.

Friendships for Virgo are typically long-lasting and based on mutual respect and shared intellectual interests. They value reliable and straightforward friends who understand Virgo's sometimes critical but well-intentioned nature. Their friends appreciate Virgo's practical advice, willingness to help, and grounded perspective.

Most Compatible Signs with Virgo:

Taurus: Earth sign Taurus complements Virgo's love for stability and practicality. This pairing is successful because of their shared values of reliability, pragmatism, and love for life's simpler pleasures. They create a grounded and harmonious relationship that values security and comfort.

Capricorn: Capricorn brings a sense of ambition and discipline that aligns well with Virgo's methodical approach. This relationship thrives on mutual respect for each other's work ethic and a shared approach to practical, long-term goals. Together, they form a partnership that is both dynamic and dependable.

Cancer: Water sign Cancer offers emotional depth and nurturing, balancing Virgo's logical nature. This pairing is successful due to Cancer's intuitive understanding of Virgo's need for order and Virgo's appreciation for Cancer's caring approach. Together, they form a nurturing and supportive bond.

Scorpio: Scorpio and Virgo love analysis and uncovering the truth. This relationship is successful because Scorpio's intensity and depth complement Virgo's attention to detail and practicality. Together, they enjoy an intellectually stimulating and sincere relationship.

Virgo finds the most fulfilling relationships with signs that offer practicality, emotional depth, and intellectual compatibility. Their ideal partnerships provide stability, mutual understanding, and a shared approach to life's intricacies.

Insights into Work and Career

- **Career Paths:** Roles that require attention to detail, organization, and analysis, such as healthcare, science, or finance, are ideal for Virgos.
- **In the Workplace:** They are efficient, organized, and often the go-to person for solving complex problems.
- **Career Tips:** Embracing flexibility and learning to manage their tendency for perfectionism can enhance Virgo's career and personal growth.

Virgo brings a meticulous, analytical, and service-oriented approach to their professional life. In their career, Virgo seeks environments that value precision, efficiency, and a pragmatic approach to problem-solving. They are characterized by a diligent work ethic, an eye for detail, and a natural inclination toward improving systems and processes.

Virgos are at their best in their careers when they can apply their keen analytical skills and attention to detail. They excel in roles that require critical thinking and a systematic approach to tasks. Their ability to dissect complex information and organize it into coherent systems is a significant asset in any analytical or administrative role.

Their service-oriented nature is another key strength. Virgo has an innate desire to be helpful and to serve, making them excellent in professions where they can aid and assist others. Whether it's through healthcare, support services, or customer relations, they find fulfillment in roles that allow them to contribute to the well-being and efficiency of others.

However, Virgos may sometimes struggle with perfectionism and self-criticism. Their high standards can make them overly critical of themselves and their work, potentially causing stress and hindering their professional growth. Learning to balance their pursuit of perfection with practicality and self-compassion can enhance their effectiveness and job satisfaction.

Most Suitable Work/Career Choices for Virgo:

Healthcare and Wellness: Virgo's meticulous nature and concern for well-being make them suited for careers in healthcare, such as nursing, pharmacy, or nutrition. Their attention to detail and caring demeanor can significantly impact the health and recovery of others.

Editorial and Writing: Virgo's precision with words and critical eye make them excellent editors or writers, particularly in technical or scientific fields. They ensure that information is communicated accurately and clearly.

Data Analysis and Research: Virgo thrives in research and data analysis roles. Their methodical approach to gathering and analyzing data makes them valuable in fields that depend on accuracy and in-depth analysis.

Project Management: Virgos excel as project managers with their organizational skills and practical mindset. They can oversee complex projects, ensuring every detail is accounted for, and objectives are met efficiently.

Environmental Sciences: Virgo's love for order and natural inclination toward conservation can lead them to careers in environmental science, where they can apply their skills to protect and manage natural resources.

Virgo excels in work environments that require precision, analytical thinking, and a service-oriented approach. They are most successful in careers that allow them to utilize their organizational strengths, detail orientation, and desire to contribute positively to their workplace and the world around them.

Famous Virgo Personalities

- **Beyoncé:** Showcases Virgo's hard work, perfectionism, and humble nature.
- **Keanu Reeves:** Reflects the modesty and depth of character typical of Virgos.
- **Mother Teresa:** Embodies Virgo's selfless service and dedication to helping others.

Virgo's meticulous nature and keen attention to detail anchor their role in the zodiac. Their practicality and analytical skills make them indispensable in both personal and professional realms, where they often serve as the bedrock of efficiency and reliability.

Chapter 9
LIBRA

Master of balance, believer in harmony, and a sucker for aesthetics.

Welcome to the harmonious world of Libra, the zodiac's epitome of balance and grace. In this chapter, we delve into the essence of Libra, represented by the scales. Known for their diplomatic nature, aesthetic sense, and strong desire for harmony, Libras are the peacemakers and art lovers of the zodiac. If you're a Libra, you'll find a reflection of your equilibrium-seeking spirit here. And if you're not, you'll gain insight into the Libra's pursuit of balance and beauty in life. From their diplomatic interactions to their love for art and culture, we'll explore what makes these air signs the embodiment of fairness and elegance.

Zodiac Birth Dates

September 23 - October 22: The time when the sun graces Libra, bringing a focus on harmony, relationships, and beauty.

Core Attributes

- **Ruling Planet:** Venus, enhancing Libra's charm, sociability, and appreciation for beauty.
- **Element:** Air, contributing to their intellectual, communicative, and social nature.
- **Symbol-The Scales:** Representing Libra's pursuit of balance, justice, and harmony in all aspects of life.

Libra, symbolized by the scales, is the zodiac sign that epitomizes balance, harmony, and fairness. Ruled by Venus, Libras are endowed with charm, sociability, and a strong appreciation for beauty and aesthetics. This Venusian influence also desires harmony in all aspects of their life, from personal relationships to their environment.

As an Air sign, Libras are intellectual, communicative, and social. They can naturally see multiple perspectives, making them excellent mediators and diplomats. Their philosophical nature drives their curiosity and interest in various subjects, especially those that involve human interactions and the arts.

The scales symbolize Libra's constant search for balance and justice. They strive to create equilibrium in every situation, often going to great lengths to avoid conflict and maintain peace. This pursuit of balance makes them fair-minded and considerate, always aiming to give equal weight to all sides of an argument or situation.

Libras are also known for their elegance and grace. They have refined tastes and often express themselves through their appearance and surroundings, favoring aesthetically pleasing and harmonious environments.

In summary, the key characteristics of Libra – their Venus-ruled charm, intellectual airiness, pursuit of balance and fairness, and a strong sense of aesthetics – combine to create a personality that is both diplomatic and artistic, always seeking harmony in the world around them.

Personality Traits

- **Diplomatic and Fair-minded:** Libras are uniquely able to see multiple sides of an issue and seek fairness.
- **Social and Charming:** They possess a natural charm and a love for social interaction, making them excellent communicators and companions.
- **Aesthetic and Artistic:** With a keen eye for beauty, Libras are drawn to artistic and cultural pursuits, appreciating and creating beauty in various forms.

Libras are defined by personality traits that align closely with their symbol, the scales, emphasizing balance, diplomacy, and a love for beauty. One of the most pronounced traits is their diplomatic and fair-minded nature. Libras have an innate ability to understand different viewpoints and strive for fairness in all their interactions. They are skilled at mediating conflicts, often acting as peacemakers in both personal and professional settings.

Social and charming, Libras thrive in group settings and enjoy engaging in meaningful conversations. Their friendly nature makes them excellent communicators, and they often have a wide circle of friends and acquaintances. Libras use their charm to be liked and to understand and connect with others, making them well-liked and approachable.

Aesthetic and artistic sensibilities are deeply ingrained in Libras. Influenced by their ruling planet Venus, they have a keen eye for beauty and harmony. This trait is reflected in their style, homes, and appreciation for art and culture. They often express themselves creatively and enjoy immersing themselves in artistic endeavors.

Despite their outward social grace, Libras are also known for their indecisiveness. Their desire to weigh all sides of a situation and avoid conflict can sometimes lead to difficulty making quick decisions. This trait stems from their pursuit of balance and fear of making the wrong choice.

Libras possess an intellectual curiosity that drives them to explore and learn about various subjects, particularly those related to human relationships and creative arts. They enjoy intellectual discussions and often seek experiences that broaden their understanding of the world.

Libra's personality traits – diplomatic, social, artistic, indecisive, and intellectually curious – paint a picture of an individual striving for balance and harmony in every aspect of life, with a strong appreciation for beauty and connection with others.

Innate Strengths

- **Mediation Skills:** Libras have a talent for resolving conflicts and bringing people together, thanks to their diplomatic nature.
- **Interpersonal Skills:** Their sociability and charm make them beloved in social circles, and they can forge and maintain strong relationships.
- **Creativity:** Libras' artistic sensibility and appreciation for beauty drive their creative talents, often excelling in artistic fields.

Libras possess a spectrum of strengths deeply rooted in their balanced and harmonious nature. One of their most notable strengths is their ability for mediation and diplomacy. Libras have an exceptional talent for understanding different perspectives and bringing about compromise. Their fair-minded approach makes them excellent at resolving conflicts and ensuring all parties feel heard and valued.

Another significant strength of Libras is their interpersonal skills. With their natural charm and sociability, they can forge strong relationships and connect with diverse people. Libras excel in social situations, using their communicative abilities to engage and enchant those around them. This makes them beloved friends, partners, and colleagues.

Creativity is also a vital aspect of Libra's strengths. The influece of Venus, the planet of beauty and art, Libras have a refined aesthetic sense and often express themselves through artistic mediums. Whether it's visual arts, music, or literature, Libras possess a unique perspective and a bring a touch of elegance to their creative pursuits.

Libras also exhibit a heightened sense of fairness and justice. They seek equality and balance in all areas of life, from their personal relationships to broader societal issues. This sense of justice often drives them to advocate for fairness and equality, making them voices for harmony and understanding.

Libras' intellectual curiosity drives them to explore and learn. They enjoy academic discussions and have a wide range of interests, often excelling in fields that require analytical thinking and a broad understanding of different subjects.

Libra's strengths – diplomatic skills, interpersonal abilities, creativity, a sense of justice, and intellectual curiosity – make them well-rounded and likable individuals, adept at navigating various aspects of life with grace and balance.

Challenges to Overcome

- **Indecisiveness:** Their desire to weigh all options can sometimes make decisions difficult.
- **Avoidance of Conflict:** While they are great at resolving conflicts, they may avoid confrontation, even when necessary.
- **Dependency on Others:** Their focus on relationships can lead to a dependency on others for validation and happiness.

Despite their many strengths, Libras also have weaknesses that stem from their deep-seated need for balance and harmony. One notable weakness is their tendency towards indecisiveness. Libras' desire to consider all sides and avoid conflict often leads to difficulty making decisions, especially when they face choices that have no clear right or wrong option. This indecisiveness can result in missed opportunities or delays in important life decisions.

Another challenge for Libras is their aversion to conflict. While they excel in resolving disputes, they may go to great lengths to avoid confrontation, even when necessary. This can lead them to suppress their needs or opinions in favor of keeping the peace, sometimes at the cost of their well-being.

Libras can also overly rely on others, especially in pursuing approval and validation. Their focus on relationships and harmony can make them dependent on the opinions and decisions of others, potentially undermining their sense of self and independence.

Furthermore, their strong sense of justice and fairness can sometimes become a preoccupation, causing them to become overly involved in the problems of others or in situations where they might not have any control. This often leads to frustration and a sense of helplessness when they cannot create harmony.

Also, Libras' love for beauty and aesthetics occasionally veers to superficiality. They might place too much emphasis on appearances in terms of their image and in judging situations or people based on superficial criteria.

Libra's challenges – indecisiveness, aversion to conflict, dependency on others, preoccupation with fairness, and a tendency towards superficiality – reflect their harmonious and balanced nature. Recognizing and addressing these areas can help Libras find a more grounded and authentic life path.

Relational Dynamics in Love and Friendship

- **Ideal Partners:** Those who can appreciate Libra's need for harmony and balance and share their love for beauty and culture.
- **Friendship Dynamics:** Libras seek intellectually stimulating friends who share similar aesthetic interests and value peace and harmony as much as they do.

Libra, known for its charm, balance, and sociability, navigates love and friendship with a desire for harmony, intellectual connection, and aesthetic appreciation. In their personal relationships, Libra seeks connections that resonate with their diplomatic nature and appreciation for beauty and fairness.

In romantic relationships, Libra is a devoted and considerate partner, often putting significant effort into maintaining harmony and balance. They are attracted to partners who can equal their intellectual prowess and share their love for the arts and beauty. A Libra in love is all about partnership and equality, often going to great lengths to ensure their relationship is stable and mutually satisfying. They thrive with partners who appreciate their need for harmony and can offer the mental stimulation they crave.

Friendships for Libra are often marked by a diverse social circle, reflecting their ability to get along with a wide range of personalities. They value communicative, fair-minded friends who share their interest in cultural and social activities. Their friends appreciate Libra's ability to bring different people together and create a harmonious social environment.

Most Compatible Signs with Libra:

Gemini: The Air sign Gemini complements Libra's intellectual and social nature. This pairing is successful because of their mutual love for conversation, social engagement, and exploring new ideas. Together, they enjoy a relationship that is intellectually enriching and socially vibrant.

Aquarius: Aquarius offers a unique and stimulating dynamic to Libra's life. This relationship thrives on intellectual stimulation and a shared desire for social justice and innovation. Aquarius' visionary nature and Libra's diplomatic skills create an exciting and socially impactful partnership.

Leo: Fire sign Leo brings passion and energy to the relationship, complementing Libra's love for harmony and beauty. This pairing is successful because Leo's charismatic nature and Libra's balancing influence create a dynamic and harmonious relationship.

Sagittarius: Sagittarius offers adventure and optimism that appeals to Libra's love for exploration and learning. This relationship is successful due to their shared love for intellectual exploration, cultural experiences, and a desire to understand the world.

Libra finds the most fulfilling relationships with signs that share their love for intellectual engagement, social harmony, and appreciation of beauty. Their ideal partnerships balance their desire for collaboration with independence and intellectual companionship.

Career Insights

- **Career Paths:** Roles that utilize Libra's mediation skills, artistic talents, or social abilities, such as law, arts, or public relations.

- **In the Workplace:** They are cooperative and harmonious colleagues, often acting as the glue that holds a team together.
- **Career Tips:** Embracing decisiveness and confronting necessary conflicts can enhance Libra's career growth and personal development.

With their inherent sense of balance and harmony, Libra brings a diplomatic and aesthetic touch to their professional life. In their career, Libra seeks roles that allow them to utilize their interpersonal skills and promote fairness and beauty. They are characterized by a natural inclination towards teamwork, a love for the arts, and a desire to create equilibrium in their work environment.

Libras excel in their careers when they can engage in partnership and collaboration. They have a unique talent for mediation and bringing people together, which makes them effective in roles that require negotiation, conflict resolution, and fostering harmonious relationships.

Their eye for aesthetics is another significant strength. Libra appreciates design and beauty, which can be effectively applied in careers related to art, fashion, interior design, or any field where a keen sense of style and presentation is valued.

However, Libras may sometimes need help with decisiveness and can become caught up in weighing options. Their desire for fairness and seeing all sides of a situation can lead to indecision. Embracing a more assertive approach and trusting their judgment can help them to make decisions more confidently.

Most Suitable Work/Career Choices for Libra:

Law and Mediation: Libra's strong sense of justice and diplomacy make them well-suited for law, mediation, or arbitration careers. They can skillfully navigate complex situations to find equitable solutions.

Design and Architecture: With their innate sense of beauty and balance, Libras thrive in design-oriented careers. They can apply their aesthetic sensibilities and creative talents to create environments or products that are both functional and appealing.

Public Relations and Communications: Libra's charm and interpersonal skills are assets in public relations and communications, where they can effectively manage relationships and craft messages that resonate with their audience.

Human Resources: Libra's ability to understand and work with different personalities makes them excellent in human resources. They can ensure that workplace dynamics are fair and that employees feel valued.

Event Planning: Libra's organizational skills and attention to detail serve them well in event planning. They can create memorable experiences that are well-coordinated and enjoyable for all participants.

Libra excels in work environments that value collaboration, aesthetics, and diplomacy. They are most successful in careers that allow them to mediate, design, communicate, and foster positive and balanced relationships.

Famous Libra Personalities

- **John Lennon:** Symbolizes Libra's artistic talent and pursuit of peace.

- **Kate Winslet:** Embodies Libra's elegance, charm, and artistic prowess.
- **Gandhi:** Reflects Libra's dedication to justice and harmonious living.

Libra's essence in the zodiac is defined by balance and harmony. Their diplomatic skills and innate sense of fairness make them adept at smoothing relationships and fostering cooperation in both personal and professional settings.

Chapter 10
SCORPIO

I'm a Scorpio, which means I'm passionate, intense, and not for the faint of heart.

D ive into the enigmatic world of Scorpio, the zodiac's symbol of depth and intensity. In this chapter, we explore the mysterious essence of Scorpio, represented by the scorpion. Known for their passionate nature, magnetic presence, and resilience, Scorpios are the transformative and powerful figures of the zodiac. If you're a Scorpio, you'll resonate with the depth and intensity highlighted here. And if you're not, you'll gain insight into Scorpio's world of mystery and strength. From their unyielding determination to their profound emotional depths, we'll uncover what makes these Water signs a force to be reckoned with.

Zodiac Birth Dates

October 23 - November 21: The period when the sun transits through Scorpio, marking a time of transformation, intensity, and deep emotional insight.

Core Attributes

- **Ruling Planets:** Mars and Pluto, endowing Scorpio with dynamic energy, deep intensity, and a focus on transformation.
- **Element:** Water, contributing to their emotional depth, intuitive insight, and magnetic charm.
- **Symbol-The Scorpion:** Symbolizing Scorpio's fearless nature, ability to survive and thrive under any circumstances, and a penchant for the mysterious.

Scorpio, symbolized by the scorpion, is a zodiac sign characterized by its intensity, depth, and transformative nature. Ruled by Mars and Pluto, Scorpios are endowed with dynamic energy and a focus on profound transformation. This dual influence combines Mars's assertiveness and Pluto's deep, reflective qualities.

Scorpios are deeply connected to the emotional and intuitive realm as a Water sign. They possess an exceptional emotional depth, allowing them to experience and understand the full spectrum of human emotions. This connection to the water element also grants them a powerful intuition and a magnetic charm that draws others to them.

The scorpion symbolizes Scorpio's fearless nature and ability to thrive and regenerate even in the most challenging circumstances. It also represents their protective and sometimes secretive demeanor, often preferring to keep their true feelings and intentions guarded.

Scorpios are known for their passion and intensity in all areas of life. They approach everything they do with a wholehearted commitment, whether it's a relationship, a career goal, or a personal endeavor. This intensity can be incredibly magnetic and charismatic, drawing others to their vital and enigmatic presence.

The key characteristics of Scorpio – their intense and transformative nature, deep emotional insight, intuitive and magnetic charm, and passionate approach to life – combine to create a personality that is both mysterious and compelling, marked by a profound ability to navigate the depths of the human experience.

Personality Traits

- **Intense and Passionate:** Scorpios are known for their depth of emotion and passionate approach to life.
- **Mysterious and Private:** They often have a mysterious aura, keeping their true feelings and thoughts guarded.

- **Resilient and Resourceful:** Scorpios possess a remarkable ability to overcome challenges and transform adversity into strength.

Scorpios are distinguished by compelling personality traits that reflect their deep, intense, and transformative nature. One of the most pronounced traits is their intensity. Scorpios approach life with a passionate and all-consuming energy. Whether in their personal relationships, careers, or hobbies, they fully immerse themselves in every endeavor.

Mysteriousness is another crucial aspect of a Scorpio's personality. They often possess an enigmatic aura, keeping their thoughts and feelings under wraps. This secrecy is not about deceit but rather a protective measure, as Scorpios only reveal their inner world to those they deeply trust.

Resilience is a defining trait of Scorpios. They have an incredible ability to withstand and overcome challenges, often emerging stronger from difficult situations. This resilience is coupled with a transformative nature, allowing Scorpios to reinvent themselves and adapt to changing circumstances.

Despite their often formidable exterior, Scorpios are profoundly emotional and sensitive. They experience emotions intensely and have a profound capacity for empathy. This emotional depth allows them to connect with others meaningfully, though they may not always show their vulnerability openly.

Scorpios are also highly intuitive. They have a knack for understanding underlying motives and unspoken feelings, making them excellent character judges. However, this intuition can also make them suspicious or wary, especially in new or unfamiliar situations.

Scorpios are fiercely loyal and protective of their loved ones. Once you earn Scorpio's trust, they are steadfast allies who will go to great lengths to support and defend you.

In essence, Scorpio's personality traits – intensity, mysteriousness, resilience, emotional depth, intuition, and loyalty – paint a picture of an individual with profound inner strength and complexity, capable of deep connections and powerful transformations.

Innate Strengths

- **Determination:** Scorpios are incredibly determined and focused, able to pursue their goals relentlessly.
- **Intuitive Insight:** Their strong intuition allows them to perceive underlying truths and motivations.
- **Loyalty:** Once committed, Scorpios are fiercely loyal and protective of their loved ones.

Scorpios possess a range of strengths that stem from their intense and transformative nature. One of their most notable strengths is their determination. Scorpios are incredibly focused and driven, able to pursue their goals with relentless dedication. This unwavering determination often enables them to achieve remarkable feats and overcome significant challenges.

Another key strength of Scorpios is their intuitive insight. They deeply understand the human psyche, often perceiving things hidden beneath the surface. This strong intuition allows them to navigate complex social dynamics. It often makes them excellent problem solvers, especially in situations requiring deep understanding of underlying motives or emotions.

Scorpios are known for their resilience and ability to transform themselves. They have a unique capacity to rise from adversity, often emerging more robust and more insightful than before. This transformative ability enables them to adapt to changing circumstances and to grow continuously throughout their lives.

Loyalty is a defining characteristic of Scorpios. Once they commit to someone, whether in a friendship, a romantic relationship, or a professional partnership, they are incredibly loyal and protective. This loyalty makes them trustworthy and dependable allies who will stand by those they care about through good times and bad.

Scorpios have a magnetic presence. Their intensity, coupled with their emotional depth, draws others to them. They often have a charismatic and compelling aura that inspires and influences those around them.

Scorpio's strengths – determination, intuitive insight, resilience, loyalty, and magnetic presence – make them powerful and influential individuals capable of deep connections and impactful achievements.

Challenges to Overcome

- **Jealousy and Possessiveness:** Their intense nature can sometimes manifest as jealousy or possessiveness in relationships.
- **Secretiveness:** While being private is a strength, it can lead to mistrust and misunderstandings.
- **Stubbornness:** Scorpios can be inflexible, sticking to their beliefs or decisions despite contrary evidence.

Despite their many strengths, Scorpios also grapple with specific weaknesses that stem from their intense and complex nature. One notable weakness is their propensity for jealousy and possessiveness, especially in personal relationships. Scorpios feel deeply, and this intensity can sometimes manifest as a fear of betrayal or loss, leading them to overly protective or controlling behaviors.

Scorpios can also be overly secretive, which, while part of their mysterious charm, can sometimes create barriers in their relationships. Their reluctance to open up and share their deeper thoughts and feelings can lead to misunderstandings and detachment from others. This secretiveness can also make it challenging for them to trust others, hindering the development of close relationships.

Another area where Scorpios may struggle is with stubbornness. They often have strong opinions and beliefs, and changing their minds can be difficult. This stubborn streak, while reflecting their determination and strength of conviction, can also limit their perspective and hinder their ability to compromise or adapt.

Scorpios' intensity can sometimes turn into an all-or-nothing attitude. They see the world in black and white, leading to extreme thinking and emotional reactions. This can make finding balance challenging and may result in emotional burnout or conflicts with others.

Their resilience and ability to transform can sometimes manifest as a tendency to hold grudges. Scorpios may find it hard to let go of past hurts or perceived wrongs, which can weigh heavily on them and affect their current relationships and well-being.

Scorpio's challenges – jealousy and possessiveness, secretiveness, stubbornness, all-or-nothing attitude, and holding grudges – reflect their deep emotional nature and intensity. Recognizing and managing these aspects can help Scorpios find a more balanced approach to their interactions and emotional life.

Relationship Dynamics in Love and Friendship

- **Ideal Partners:** Those who appreciate Scorpio's depth and can handle their intensity, such as fellow Water signs Cancer and Pisces or Earth signs like Capricorn and Taurus.
- **Friendship Dynamics:** Scorpios value deep, meaningful friendships based on trust and mutual respect.

Renowned for their intensity and depth, Scorpio approaches relationships with a blend of passion, loyalty, and a desire for profound emotional connections. In love and friendship, Scorpio seeks connections that resonate with their profound sense of understanding and a shared appreciation for the deeper aspects of life.

In romantic relationships, Scorpio is intensely devoted and passionate. They are attracted to partners who can connect with them deeply emotionally and appreciate the complexity of their feelings. A Scorpio in love is about depth, commitment, and transformative experiences. They thrive in relationships that offer emotional intimacy and a sense of shared secrets and discoveries. Their ideal partners are those willing to explore the depths of emotion and handle the intensity that comes with a Scorpio's love.

In friendships, Scorpio is a fiercely loyal and protective companion. They value friendships based on mutual trust, honesty, and emotional depth. Scorpio friends are the ones who will stand by you in the most challenging times, offering unwavering support and a deep understanding of your emotional needs. They appreciate friends who respect their privacy and are unafraid to delve into meaningful and sometimes challenging conversations.

Most Compatible Signs with Scorpio:

Cancer: Fellow Water sign Cancer shares Scorpio's depth of emotion and desire for emotional security. This pairing is successful due to their mutual understanding of each other's emotional needs and desire to build a deeply connected and nurturing relationship.

Pisces: Pisces complement Scorpio's intensity with their empathetic and intuitive nature. This relationship is successful because of their shared emotional depth, intuitive understanding, and mutual appreciation for life's mystical and spiritual aspects.

Virgo: Earth sign Virgo offers a practical and analytical balance to Scorpio's emotional intensity. This relationship is successful due to Virgo's ability to provide a grounding influence while appreciating Scorpio's depth, resulting in an emotionally enriching and practically supportive partnership.

Capricorn: Capricorn brings stability and ambition that align well with Scorpio's determination and intensity. This pairing works well because of their shared values of loyalty, commitment, and drive to achieve mutual goals.

Scorpio finds the most fulfilling relationships with signs that offer emotional depth, understanding, and a willingness to explore the complexities of the human psyche. Their ideal partnerships provide a solid emotional bond, mutual trust, and a shared journey through life's more profound mysteries.

Career Insights

- **Career Paths:** Roles that require strategic thinking, problem-solving, and the ability to handle complex challenges, such as research, investigation, or crisis management.

- **In the Workplace:** Scorpios are dedicated and committed, often thriving in high-pressure environments.
- **Professional Development:** Embracing flexibility and openness can enhance Scorpio's career growth and interpersonal relationships.

Recognized for their intensity and depth, Scorpio approaches their professional life with a focus on transformation, investigation, and a strong desire for mastery. In their career, Scorpio values roles that challenge them intellectually, allow for deep analysis, and provide the opportunity to exercise control and influence. They are known for their strategic thinking, resourcefulness, and unwavering commitment to their goals.

Scorpios are at their best in careers that engage their investigative nature. They have a keen eye for uncovering the truth and delving into complex problems, making them well-suited for roles in research, forensic science, or any field that requires digging beneath the surface.

Their determination and resilience are also significant strengths in the workplace. Scorpios are not afraid of challenges or hard work; they are the ones who stay committed to a task long after others might give up. Their passion for their work can lead to significant achievements and breakthroughs in their chosen field.

However, Scorpios may sometimes struggle with flexibility and letting go of control. Their preference for being in charge can sometimes become a need for power, creating conflicts, especially in team environments. Learning to balance their strong will with collaboration can enhance their professional relationships and success.

Most Suitable Work/Career Choices for Scorpio:

Criminology and Law Enforcement: Scorpio's investigative skills and passion for uncovering the truth make them excellent in criminology and law enforcement. They are tenacious in their pursuit of justice and can precisely navigate complex criminal cases.

Psychology and Counseling: Scorpio's depth and understanding of human nature serve them well in psychology or counseling, where they can help others through transformative personal challenges.

Finance and Investment: Scorpio's strategic mind and attention to detail make them well-suited for careers in finance and investment. They have the insight and patience to navigate the complexities of financial systems and make calculated informed decisions.

Research and Development: Scorpio's ability to concentrate and delve into the heart of complex matters makes them valuable in research and development, where thorough analysis and innovation are fundamental.

Corporate Strategy: With their strategic approach and determination, Scorpios excel in corporate strategy roles, helping to steer companies through competitive markets and toward long-term success.

In summary, Scorpio excels in work environments that offer depth, complexity, and the opportunity for significant influence. They are most successful in careers that leverage their investigative nature, strategic thinking, and unwavering determination to achieve profound and impactful results.

Famous Scorpio Personalities

- **Bill Gates:** Exemplifies Scorpio's strategic mind and determination.
- **Julia Roberts:** Reflects the depth and charisma typical of Scorpios.
- **Leonardo DiCaprio:** A testament to Scorpio's intensity and passion for their craft.

Scorpio brings intensity and depth to the zodiac. Their powerful emotional insights and unwavering focus make them influential in personal and professional realms, often acting as the catalysts for transformation and profound understanding.

Chapter 11
SAGITTARIUS

Where 'freedom' is the motto and 'explorer' is the identity.

L et's journey with Sagittarius, the zodiac's free spirit and truth seeker. In this chapter, we explore the expansive world of Sagittarius, symbolized by the archer. Known for their love of freedom, optimism, and thirst for knowledge, Sagittarians are the adventurers and philosophers of the zodiac. If you're a Sagittarius, your adventurous and curious spirit will be reflected in these pages. For those who aren't, this chapter offers a window into the Sagittarian pursuit of growth, exploration, and understanding. From their boundless enthusiasm to their philosophical outlook, we'll discover what makes these fire signs the epitome of the eternal traveler and learner.

Zodiac Birth Dates

November 22 - December 21: The period when the sun transits through Sagittarius, bringing a time of exploration, adventure, and the pursuit of knowledge and truth.

Core Attributes

- **Ruling Planet:** Jupiter, endowing Sagittarius with optimism, love for freedom, and a quest for knowledge.
- **Element:** Fire, contributing to their dynamic energy, enthusiasm, and exploratory spirit.
- **Symbol-The Archer:** Representing Sagittarius's aim for higher knowledge, exploration, and the desire to venture beyond the known.

Sagittarius, symbolized by the archer, is known for its adventurous, optimistic, and freedom-loving nature. Ruled by Jupiter, the most giant planet in the solar system, Sagittarians are endowed with a sense of expansiveness and a quest for knowledge and truth. This Jupiterian influence imparts an inherent optimism, a desire for exploration, and a penchant for philosophy.

As a Fire sign, Sagittarians possess dynamic energy, enthusiasm, and an exploratory spirit. They are often seen as the adventurers of the zodiac, always seeking new experiences and horizons. This fiery nature drives their passion for life and fuels their adventurous endeavors.

The symbol of the archer represents Sagittarius's aim for higher understanding, exploration, and the desire to venture beyond the known. It signifies their quest for knowledge and truth, both in the literal sense of travel and exploration and in the metaphorical sense of intellectual and spiritual seeking.

Sagittarians are characterized by their free-spirited approach to life. They value their freedom highly and often resist anything that feels like a constraint on their independence. This love of liberty combines a natural curiosity and a desire to understand the world and its myriad cultures, philosophies, and belief systems.

The core attributes of Sagittarius – their Jupiter-ruled optimism, fiery energy, adventurous nature, quest for knowledge, and love for freedom – combine to create a personality that is constantly seeking, always exploring, and always aiming for a higher understanding of the world around them.

Personality Traits

- **Adventurous and Free-spirited:** Sagittarians are known for their love of travel, exploration, and experiencing new cultures and ideas.
- **Optimistic and Enthusiastic:** They possess a naturally positive outlook and an infectious enthusiasm for new experiences.
- **Philosophical and Intellectual:** Sagittarians are often deep thinkers interested in exploring philosophical and

intellectual pursuits.

Sagittarians are defined by vibrant personality traits that reflect their adventurous and philosophical nature. One of their most pronounced traits is their adventurous and free-spirited nature. Sagittarians love to explore, whether it's through physical travel, intellectual pursuits, or by immersing themselves in different cultures and ideas. Their love for adventure extends to a willingness to take risks and try new things, often leading them to a rich and varied life experience.

Optimism is another crucial aspect of Sagittarius's personality. They possess a naturally positive outlook and often see the silver lining in difficult situations. This optimism fuels their enthusiasm for life and belief that anything is possible.

Sagittarians are also known for their intellectual and philosophical inclinations. They are curious about the world and often pursue a lifelong quest for knowledge and understanding. This thirst for learning can make them excellent conversationalists, always ready to discuss new ideas or share insights.

Despite their outgoing nature, Sagittarians can sometimes be quite blunt. Their honesty is generally well-intentioned, but they may unintentionally hurt others' feelings with their directness. Learning to temper their frankness with tact is often a key area of personal growth.

Lastly, Sagittarians have a strong sense of independence. They value their freedom highly and often resist constraints or obligations that limit their autonomy. This love for independence is both a strength and a challenge, as it fuels their adventurous spirit but can also lead to issues in relationships where compromise is necessary.

Sagittarius's personality traits – adventurousness, optimism, intellectual curiosity, honesty, and independence – paint a picture of an individual who is always looking forward, eager to explore and understand the world, and unafraid to speak their mind.

Innate Strengths

- **Adaptability:** Sagittarians are highly adaptable and can quickly embrace change and new opportunities.
- **Curiosity:** Their quest for knowledge and understanding drives them to explore various subjects and ideas.
- **Inspirational:** Their optimism and zest for life often inspire and uplift those around them.

Sagittarians possess a range of strengths deeply rooted in their adventurous, optimistic, and intellectual nature. One of their most notable strengths is their adaptability. Sagittarians are incredibly flexible and open to change, able to adjust to new situations easily and enthusiastically. This adaptability makes them resilient despite life's unpredictability and opens them to various experiences.

Another key strength is their insatiable curiosity. Sagittarians have a thirst for knowledge and understanding that drives them to explore various subjects and ideas. This quest for learning broadens their horizons and makes them well-rounded and insightful individuals.

Their natural optimism is a powerful asset. Sagittarians can maintain a positive outlook, even in challenging circumstances. This positivity is uplifting for themselves and those around them, making them sources of inspiration and encouragement.

Sagittarians are also known for their inspirational qualities. Their enthusiasm for life and adventurous spirit often helps others to step out of their comfort zones and embrace new opportunities. They are often seen as role models for living life to the fullest.

A Sagittarian's philosophical outlook gives them a unique perspective on life. They often see the bigger picture and can make connections between different experiences and ideas. This philosophical nature leads them to meaningful insights and a deeper understanding of life.

Sagittarius's strengths – adaptability, curiosity, optimism, inspirational qualities, and a philosophical outlook – make them dynamic and engaging individuals, always eager to explore the world and share their joy and knowledge with others.

Challenges to Overcome

- **Impatience:** Their desire for constant movement and change can sometimes lead to impatience and restlessness.
- **Over-optimism:** Their positive outlook can sometimes be unrealistic, leading them to overlook practical details.
- **Tendency to Overcommit:** Their enthusiasm often leads them to take on more than they can handle, resulting in scattered energies.

Despite their many positive attributes, Sagittarians also have weaknesses that stem from their freedom-loving and expansive nature. One significant weakness is their tendency towards impatience. Their desire for constant movement and exploration can sometimes make them restless and easily frustrated with situations that require patience and steady progress.

Another area where Sagittarians struggle is their over-optimism. While their positive outlook is generally a strength, it can sometimes lead them to overlook practical details or underestimate challenges. This over-optimism can result in unrealistic expectations or underpreparedness for life's complexities.

Sagittarians can also have a tendency to overcommit. Their enthusiasm and desire to experience everything can lead them to take on more than they can realistically handle. This can result in them spreading their energies too thin and needing help to follow through on all their commitments.

While admirable, their straightforward and honest nature can sometimes border on tactlessness. Sagittarians value truth and directness but may inadvertently hurt others with their blunt words or fail to recognize when diplomacy is needed.

Their strong sense of independence and dislike for constraints can sometimes manifest as a reluctance to settle down or commit, whether in relationships, careers, or other areas of life. This can be challenging for Sagittarians who seek deeper connections or long-term stability but need help to balance this with their need for freedom.

Sagittarius's weaknesses – impatience, over-optimism, tendency to overcommit, tactlessness, and a reluctance to settle down – reflect their adventurous and free-spirited nature. Recognizing and addressing these aspects can help Sagittarians find a more balanced and fulfilling approach to their pursuits and relationships.

Relationship Dynamics in Love and Friendship

- **Ideal Partners:** Those who can match Sagittarius's adventurous spirit and intellectual curiosity and value freedom and growth.

- **Friendship Dynamics:** Sagittarians seek friends who are open-minded, adventurous, and willing to explore life's many possibilities.

Sagittarius, known for their adventurous spirit and philosophical mind, navigates love and friendship with enthusiasm, honesty, and a thirst for exploration. Sagittarius seeks connections that resonate with their passion for adventure and intellectual curiosity in their personal relationships.

In romantic relationships, Sagittarius is a partner who values freedom, growth, and shared adventures. They are attracted to those who can match their zest for life and are open to exploring the world's vast possibilities together. A Sagittarius in love is spontaneous and open-hearted. It often seeks a relationship that is not just romantic but also a journey of shared learning and exploration. They thrive with partners who respect their need for independence and are enthusiastic about life's adventures.

In the sphere of friendships, Sagittarius is the quintessential companion for travel, intellectual debates, and spontaneous plans. They value friends who are open-minded, who enjoy lively discussions, and who are willing to embark on new adventures. Their friends appreciate Sagittarius's straightforwardness, infectious optimism, and the excitement they bring to every encounter.

Most Compatible Signs with Sagittarius:

Aries: Fellow Fire sign Aries shares Sagittarius's enthusiasm for life and adventure. This pairing is successful due to their mutual energy, love for exploration, and a shared desire for independence. They enjoy a dynamic and exciting relationship filled with new experiences and adventures.

Leo: Leo complements Sagittarius's adventurous spirit with their charismatic and warm-hearted nature. This relationship thrives on mutual admiration and a love for the grandeur of life. Both signs appreciate each other's passion, creating a partnership that is both vibrant and full of joy.

Aquarius: The Air sign Aquarius offers a unique and intellectual match to Sagittarius's philosophical nature. This pairing is successful because of their shared love for learning, exploration, and challenging the status quo. Together, they form an intellectually stimulating relationship and respect each partner's need for freedom and space.

Libra: Libra brings a sense of balance and harmony to Sagittarius's life. This relationship is successful due to Libra's ability to appreciate Sagittarius's adventurous nature while offering a more grounded and diplomatic perspective. Together, they enjoy an intellectually enriching and socially engaging partnership.

Sagittarius finds the most fulfilling relationships with signs that share their love for adventure, intellectual exploration, and freedom. Their ideal partnerships balance their desire for independence with mutual understanding and appreciation.

Career Insights

- **Career Paths:** Roles that offer variety, intellectual stimulation, and opportunities for exploration, such as travel, education, or entrepreneurship.
- **In the Workplace:** They are enthusiastic and creative colleagues, often bringing fresh perspectives and innovative ideas.
- **Career Tips:** Focusing on patience and practicality can enhance Sagittarius's career growth and effectiveness.

Sagittarians, known for their adventurous spirit and quest for knowledge, bring unique qualities to their professional lives. Their natural inclination for exploration and intellectual curiosity shapes their approach to work and career choices. Sagittarians thrive in environments that offer freedom, variety, and opportunities for personal and intellectual growth.

One of Sagittarius's significant strengths in the workplace is their adaptability. They excel in dynamic environments, readily embracing change and new challenges. Their optimistic outlook and ability to see the bigger picture help them navigate workplace complexities with ease and enthusiasm.

Their love for learning and exploration makes them lifelong learners, always eager to expand their knowledge and skills. This trait makes them valuable assets in roles that require staying updated with the latest trends, research, or technologies.

However, Sagittarians may struggle with routine or mundane tasks, preferring roles that offer variety and excitement. Their need for freedom and independence can sometimes be at odds with structured environments. Finding a balance between their adventurous spirit and the demands of their role is critical to their professional satisfaction.

Most Suitable Work/Career Choices for Sagittarius:

Travel Guide or Travel Writer: Sagittarians' love for adventure and exploration makes them perfect for careers in travel. Their talent for adapting to new cultures and environments and their storytelling skills allow them to excel as travel guides or writers, sharing their experiences with a broader audience.

Educator or Academic: With their passion for knowledge and intellectual curiosity, Sagittarians are well-suited for academic or educational roles. Their enthusiasm for learning is infectious, making them inspiring teachers or professors who can engage and motivate their students.

Entrepreneur: Sagittarians' adaptability, vision, and independence make entrepreneurship a fitting career choice. They thrive when free to pursue innovative ideas and bring them to fruition, often leading them to success in their entrepreneurial ventures.

Marketing or Public Relations Professional: These fields require creativity, adaptability, and excellent communication skills, which are Sagittarian strengths. Their goft for engaging with diverse audiences and their innovative approach to problem-solving make them successful in marketing or PR roles.

Outdoor Adventure Leader: Sagittarians' love for the outdoors and their adventurous nature make them ideal for roles in outdoor recreation. Whether as adventure sports instructors, guides, or conservationists, they find fulfillment in careers that connect them with nature and allow them to share their passion with others.

In summary, Sagittarians bring enthusiasm, adaptability, and a thirst for knowledge to their work and career. They excel in professions that align with their love for freedom, exploration, and intellectual growth, succeeding in roles that allow them to utilize these inherent qualities.

Famous Sagittarius Personalities

- **Brad Pitt:** Reflects Sagittarius's charm, adventurous spirit, and intellectual curiosity.
- **Taylor Swift:** Embodies Sagittarius's optimism, creativity, and exploratory nature.
- **Mark Twain:** A testament to Sagittarius's love for storytelling, travel, and philosophical insight.

Sagittarius infuses the zodiac with their adventurous spirit and philosophical mind. Their love for exploration and quest for knowledge inspire growth and excitement in both personal and professional realms, making them natural motivators and visionaries.

Chapter 12
CAPRICORN

Where hardworking is an understatement and success a foregone conclusion.

S tep into the world of Capricorn, the zodiac's emblem of discipline and ambition. In this chapter, we uncover the steadfast nature of Capricorn, represented by the mountain goat. Known for their resilience, practicality, and strong work ethic, Capricorns are the planners and achievers of the zodiac. If you're a Capricorn, these pages will echo your determination and pragmatic approach to life. For others, it offers an insight into the Capricorn's journey of hard work, discipline, and aspiration. From their commitment to goals to their structured and methodical way of life, we'll explore what makes these earth signs the epitome of persistence and reliability.

Zodiac Birth Dates

December 22 - January 19: The period when the sun moves through Capricorn, marking a time of practical ambition, disciplined achievement, and steady progress.

Core Attributes

- **Ruling Planet:** Saturn, giving Capricorn a sense of responsibility, structure, and discipline.
- **Element:** Earth, grounding them in practicality, realism, and a results-oriented approach.
- **Symbol-The Mountain Goat:** Symbolic of Capricorn's perseverance, ability to navigate challenges, and ambition to reach the summit.

Capricorn, symbolized by the mountain goat, is known for its discipline, ambition, and practical nature. Saturn, the planet of responsibility and structure, rules Capricorn, empowering them with a strong sense of duty, determination, and a drive for achievement. This Saturnian influence instills in them a seriousness and an ability to persevere through challenges.

As an Earth sign, Capricorns are grounded, realistic, and results-oriented. They possess a pragmatic approach to life, focusing on tangible outcomes and long-term goals. This earthiness manifests itself as a strong work ethic and a preference for stability and order.

The symbol of the mountain goat represents Capricorn's ability to navigate challenging terrains and steadily climb towards their goals. It signifies their persistence, resilience, and capacity to rise to the top through hard work and determination.

Capricorns are characterized by their systematic and structured approach. They plan meticulously and execute their strategies precisely, making them excellent organizers and managers. Their disciplined nature ensures they stay focused and committed to their objectives, often achieving high success.

The key characteristics of Capricorn – their Saturn-ruled discipline, earthy pragmatism, goal-oriented nature, and structured approach – combine to create a personality that is steadfast, ambitious, and capable of overcoming any obstacle to achieve their aspirations.

Personality Traits

- **Disciplined and Structured:** Capricorns are known for their self-control, systematic approach, and strong discipline in all aspects of life.
- **Practical and Realistic:** They have a pragmatic approach to problem-solving and decision-making, preferring practical solutions over theoretical ones.

- **Ambitious and Determined:** Capricorns are driven by their goals and aspirations, often exhibiting a strong work ethic and an unwavering commitment to their objectives.

Capricorns are marked by defining personality traits that reflect their disciplined, ambitious, and pragmatic nature. One of the most prominent traits is their disciplined and structured approach to life. Capricorns are known for their self-control and ability to manage time and resources efficiently. They approach tasks and challenges methodically, often adhering to traditional and proven strategies.

Practicality and realism are vital aspects of a Capricorn's personality. They prefer tangible, real-world solutions and are often grounded in their approach to problem-solving. This practical mindset makes them cautious and conservative in their decisions, constantly weighing the long-term implications before acting.

Ambition is a driving force for Capricorns. They are goal-oriented and clearly envision what they want to achieve. Their determination and persistence in pursuing these goals often lead to significant achievements in their personal and professional lives.

Despite their serious demeanor, Capricorns possess a subtle, dry sense of humor. They can be surprisingly witty and have a unique way of observing and commenting on the world around them.

However, their disciplined nature can sometimes come across as rigid or overly conservative. Capricorns might find adapting to new or unconventional ideas challenging, preferring to stick to what is tried and tested.

Capricorns also tend to be reserved and cautious in expressing their emotions. They value privacy and often build a wall around their inner world, only opening up to those they trust deeply.

Capricorn's personality traits – discipline, practicality, ambition, dry humor, conservatism, and emotional reserve – paint a picture of an individual who is steadfast, focused, and deeply committed to their goals, yet with an underlying complexity and depth of character.

Innate Strengths

- **Resilience:** Capricorns have an incredible ability to withstand challenges and persist in facing obstacles, making them remarkably resilient.
- **Strategic Planning:** Their methodical approach and foresight enable them to plan effectively and achieve long-term success.
- **Reliability:** Capricorns are dependable and trustworthy, often seen as anchors in personal and professional settings.

Capricorns possess a range of strengths that stem from their disciplined, pragmatic, and ambitious nature. One of their most notable strengths is their resilience. Capricorns can withstand and overcome challenges, often using adversity as a stepping stone to reach their goals. This resilience and unwavering determination enable them to achieve impressive feats of endurance and success.

Another key strength of Capricorns is their strategic planning and organizational skills. Their systematic approach and foresight allow them to effectively plan and execute long-term projects and goals. They are excellent at breaking down complex tasks into manageable steps, ensuring steady progress and completion.

Capricorns are also known for their reliability and trustworthiness. They take their commitments seriously and are often the ones others turn to for stability and dependability. Whether in personal relationships or professional settings, they are seen as pillars of strength, consistently delivering on their promises.

Their practicality is another significant asset. Capricorns are adept at making realistic assessments and grounded decisions. This pragmatic mindset allows them to navigate life with a clear sense of reality, making sound choices based on practical considerations.

Lastly, Capricorns possess a strong work ethic. They are hardworking and dedicated, often going above and beyond. This dedication is not just about achieving success but also about fulfilling their sense of responsibility and duty.

Capricorn's strengths – resilience, strategic planning, reliability, practicality, and a strong work ethic – make them formidable and respected individuals. They excel in situations that require discipline, structure, and a long-term approach, bringing stability and order to their endeavors.

Challenges to Overcome

- **Tendency to be Pessimistic:** Their realistic outlook can sometimes veer into pessimism, causing them to focus more on the potential negatives than the positives.
- **Inflexibility:** Capricorns can resist change and new ideas, preferring to stick to tried and true methods.
- **Workaholic Nature:** Their strong work ethic can sometimes lead to overworking and neglecting other aspects of life.

While Capricorns possess numerous strengths, they also have weaknesses that stem from their disciplined and pragmatic nature. One of the main weaknesses of Capricorns is their tendency to be pessimistic. While beneficial in many ways, their realistic outlook can sometimes lead them to focus more on the potential negatives and overlook the positives. This pessimism can dampen their own spirits and those of people around them.

Another area where Capricorns might need help is inflexibility. Their preference for structure and tried-and-true methods can make them resistant to change and new ideas. This rigidity can hinder their adaptability and ability to embrace new opportunities or innovative solutions.

Capricorns can also be prone to overworking. Their strong work ethic and ambition might lead them to take on excessive responsibilities, often at the expense of their personal life and well-being. This workaholic nature can lead to stress and burnout, impacting their overall health and happiness.

Their reserved and cautious nature in expressing emotions can sometimes come across as cold or unapproachable. Capricorns may find it challenging to openly express affection or vulnerability, creating barriers to forming close personal relationships.

Capricorn's strong desire for control and perfection can sometimes manifest as micromanagement in professional settings or needing things done a certain way, which can be off-putting to others who value autonomy and creativity.

Capricorn's challenges – a tendency toward pessimism, inflexibility, overworking, emotional reserve, and a need for control – reflect their disciplined and goal-oriented nature. Recognizing and addressing these aspects can help Capricorns find a more balanced approach to their personal and professional lives.

Relationship Dynamics in Love and Friendship

- **Ideal Partners:** Those who understand Capricorn's dedication and support their ambitions, such as fellow Earth signs Taurus and Virgo or Water signs like Scorpio and Pisces.
- **Friendship Dynamics:** Capricorns value friendships based on mutual respect, shared goals, and a sense of reliability.

With their disciplined and pragmatic approach to life, Capricorns seek relationships that offer stability, mutual respect, and shared goals. Their approach to love and friendships is marked by loyalty, sincerity, and a preference for meaningful, long-term connections.

In romantic relationships, Capricorns are dedicated and serious partners. They value stability, mutual support, and a shared vision for the future. They are drawn to partners who are equally ambitious, responsible, and who appreciate the importance of hard work and commitment. However, Capricorns also need a partner who can understand their reserved nature and respect their need for personal space and independence.

In friendships, Capricorns are reliable and loyal. They value friendships built on trust, mutual respect, and shared values. They prefer a smaller circle of close friends over a vast network of acquaintances. Their friends appreciate their wisdom, practical advice, and unwavering support.

Most Compatible Signs with Capricorn:

Taurus: This Earth sign pairing is successful due to their shared values of stability, practicality, and a love for the finer things in life. Capricorn and Taurus appreciate hard work and are committed to building a secure and comfortable life. Their mutual understanding of each other's need for stability and security creates a harmonious and enduring relationship.

Virgo: Another Earth sign, Virgo complements Capricorn's practical and disciplined nature with their meticulous and analytical approach. This pairing is successful because both signs value efficiency, responsibility, and a systematic approach to life. They work well together, creating a well-organized and harmonious relationship built on shared respect and shared goals.

Pisces: As a Water sign, Pisces pairs well with Capricorn by bringing emotional depth and intuition to balance Capricorn's practicality. This relationship is successful because Pisces' compassionate and artistic nature complements Capricorn's structure and stability. Pisces helps Capricorn to open up emotionally, while Capricorn provides a grounding influence for Pisces.

Capricorn's compatibility in love and friendships revolves around shared values of loyalty, responsibility, and practicality. Relationships that offer stability, mutual support, and respect for each other's ambitions will likely thrive with a Capricorn.

Career Insights

- **Career Paths:** Roles that require strategic planning, leadership, and a detail-oriented approach, such as management, finance, or law.
- **In the Workplace:** Capricorns are diligent and focused professionals, often taking on leadership roles and driving projects to completion.
- **Career Tips:** Embracing adaptability and work-life balance can enhance Capricorn's career growth and well-

being.

Capricorns, with their disciplined, ambitious, and practical nature, bring distinctive qualities to their professional lives. Their approach to work and career is often characterized by a strong work ethic, a strategic mindset, and a focus on long-term goals. Capricorns excel in environments that require structure, discipline, and steady progression toward defined objectives.

One of Capricorn's greatest strengths in the workplace is their ability to plan and strategize effectively. They are excellent at setting long-term goals and devising detailed plans to achieve them. Their methodical approach ensures that they stay on track and consistently make progress.

Their discipline and dedication make them reliable and hardworking professionals. Capricorns are fearless in putting in the extra effort to ensure their work meets the highest standards. This reliability and attention to detail often make them invaluable team members.

However, Capricorns may sometimes struggle with flexibility. Their preference for structure and proven methods can make adapting to new and unconventional approaches challenging. Embracing adaptability and being open to innovative ideas can enhance their professional effectiveness.

Most Suitable Work/Career Choices for Capricorn:

Management or Executive Roles: Capricorns' strategic thinking, reliability, and planning ability make them well-suited for leadership positions. Their natural inclination towards structure and order, combined with their ambition, allows them to excel in managerial or executive roles where they can guide teams and projects towards success.

Finance or Accounting: Capricorns' detail-oriented and methodical nature aligns well with careers in finance or accounting. Their precision, coupled with a pragmatic approach to problem-solving, enables them to excel in roles that require financial planning, analysis, or management of resources.

Law or Legal Professions: Capricorns' respect for rules and structure and their analytical skills make them suited for the legal field. Whether as lawyers, legal analysts, or judges, they can navigate complex legal systems and provide well-reasoned, structured arguments.

Engineering: The practical and problem-solving aspects of engineering align with Capricorn's logical and systematic approach. Their ability to focus on details and work systematically makes them successful in various engineering disciplines.

Entrepreneurship: Although it might seem counterintuitive, Capricorns can be successful entrepreneurs due to their disciplined approach and resilience. They can build businesses with a strong foundation and a clear long-term vision, navigating the challenges of entrepreneurship with determination and practicality.

Capricorns bring a strategic, disciplined, and practical approach to their work and career. They thrive in professions that allow them to utilize their strengths in planning, organization, and goal-oriented execution, achieving success through their steadfast commitment and meticulous approach.

Famous Capricorn Personalities

- **Michelle Obama:** Exemplifies Capricorn's discipline, intelligence, and strong sense of duty.
- **Jeff Bezos:** Reflects Capricorn's ambition, strategic thinking, and drive for success.
- **Kate Middleton:** A testament to Capricorn's elegance, responsibility, and commitment to their roles.

Capricorn stands as a symbol of discipline and ambition in the zodiac. Their practical approach and unwavering determination make them pillars of strength and reliability in personal and professional realms, often driving them to achieve and lead with remarkable resilience.

Chapter 13
AQUARIUS

In my world convention is questioned and the future is invented every day.

Experience the world of Aquarius, the zodiac's symbol of innovation and uniqueness. In this chapter, we delve into the essence of Aquarius, represented by the water bearer. Known for their originality, intellectualism, and humanitarian spirit, Aquarians are the visionaries and trailblazers of the zodiac. If you're an Aquarius, these pages will mirror your innovative and unconventional spirit. For those who aren't, this chapter offers an insight into Aquarius's journey of breaking norms, embracing new ideas, and striving for social progress. From their penchant for thinking outside the box to their commitment to improving the world, we'll explore what makes these air signs the epitome of originality and progressiveness.

Zodiac Birth Dates

January 20 - February 18: The period when the sun transits through Aquarius, marking a time of intellectual exploration, social innovation, and a drive for humanitarian change.

Core Attributes

- **Ruling Planets:** Uranus and Saturn, endowing Aquarius with a blend of revolutionary thinking, intellect, and a disciplined approach to societal change.
- **Element:** Air, contributing to their intellectual, communicative, and social nature.
- **Symbol-The Water Bearer:** Representing Aquarius's role as the bearer of new ideas and humanitarian ideals.

Aquarius, symbolized by the water bearer, is known for its progressive, innovative, and humanitarian nature. Aquarians are ruled by Uranus, the planet of revolution and change. Aquarians have a visionary outlook, a strong sense of individuality, and a drive to challenge the status quo. This Uranian influence fosters a forward-thinking and unconventional approach to life.

As an Air sign, Aquarians are intellectual, communicative, and socially oriented. They possess a natural ability for abstract thinking and often explore new ideas and concepts. This philosophical bent is often directed towards social and technological advancements, highlighting their role as thinkers and innovators.

The symbol of the water bearer represents Aquarius's role in bringing forth new ideas and nurturing societal progress. It signifies their humanitarian spirit and desire to contribute to the betterment of society. Aquarians are often driven by a deep sense of social justice and a desire to make the world more equitable and advanced.

Aquarians are characterized by their originality and nonconformity. They pride themselves on being different and are not afraid to stand out from the crowd. This uniqueness is coupled with a strong sense of independence; they are not ones to follow the herd and prefer to carve their own path.

The core attributes of Aquarius – their Uranus-ruled innovation, air sign intellectuality, humanitarian nature, and distinctive individuality – combine to create a visionary and eccentric personality, always looking towards the future and striving to make a meaningful impact on the world.

Personality Traits

- **Innovative and Original:** Aquarians are known for their unique perspective and inventive ideas. They are often ahead of their time, thinking in ways that challenge conventional norms.

- **Intellectual and Analytical**: Aquarians are deep thinkers with a natural inclination towards intellectual pursuits, often exploring complex ideas and theories.
- **Humanitarian and Altruistic:** They have a desire to contribute to the betterment of humanity and a strong sense of social justice, often involved in social causes and community work.

Aquarians are defined by a unique personality trait set that reflects their innovative, independent, and humanitarian nature. One of the most pronounced traits is their originality and nonconformity. Aquarians value their uniqueness and often have a distinct way of thinking and approaching life. They are not afraid to challenge conventional norms and are often seen as trendsetters or trailblazers in their communities.

Intellectually curious and analytical, Aquarians have a natural inclination towards intellectual pursuits. They are deep thinkers, often exploring complex ideas and theories. This intellectualism is not just theoretical; they often seek to apply their ideas in ways that can bring about social or technological change.

Aquarians are also known for their humanitarianism. They have a strong sense of social justice and often engage in causes that aim to improve the world. Their altruistic nature drives them to contribute positively to society through innovative ideas, community work, or activism.

Despite their social nature, Aquarians can sometimes be emotionally detached or aloof. They value their independence highly and may prefer to keep a certain distance in their personal relationships. This detachment is more about preserving their individuality and less about a lack of empathy.

Their forward-thinking nature can sometimes manifest as a tendency to be ahead of their time. Aquarians often have ideas or perspectives that others might not readily understand or accept, sometimes making them feel isolated or out of sync with their surroundings.

Aquarius's personality traits – originality, intellectual curiosity, humanitarianism, emotional detachment, and a forward-thinking approach – paint a picture of an individual who is both visionary and unconventional, always seeking to explore new ideas and make a meaningful contribution to the world.

Innate Strengths

- **Creativity:** Aquarians possess a highly creative and imaginative mind, often coming up with unconventional solutions to problems.
- **Independence:** They value their independence and autonomy and are not afraid to chart their own course in life.
- **Social Awareness:** With a keen interest in social issues, Aquarians are often at the forefront of efforts to bring about positive change.

Aquarians possess a set of strengths that align closely with their visionary and humanitarian nature. One of the most significant strengths of Aquarius is its creativity and innovation. Their ability to think outside the box and develop original ideas sets them apart. This innovative mindset often leads them to propose new and unconventional solutions to problems, making them valuable in fields that require creative thinking.

Another key strength is their intellectualism. Aquarians have a natural affinity for learning and exploring various subjects, especially social change, technology, and future possibilities. Their intellectual curiosity broadens their horizons and enables them to contribute insightful perspectives to any discussion or project.

Aquarians are also known for their strong sense of social justice and humanitarianism. They are often driven by a desire to improve the world through activism, volunteer work, or simply by spreading awareness about important issues. Their altruism and empathy make them effective in roles that require compassion and a deep understanding of social dynamics.

Independence is another notable strength of Aquarians. They follow their own path and value their freedom and autonomy, rather than conforming to societal expectations. This independence of thought and action allows them to pioneer new ideas and approaches.

Aquarians possess strong communication skills. They are often articulate and able to express their innovative ideas clearly. Communicating effectively is essential in bringing others on board with their visionary projects and ideals.

In summary, Aquarius's strengths – creativity, intellectual curiosity, humanitarianism, independence, and communication skills – make them unique and forward-thinking individuals. They excel in environments that value innovation, social change, and intellectual exploration.

Challenges to Overcome

- **Detachment:** Aquarians can sometimes be emotionally detached or aloof, hindering close personal relationships.
- **Stubbornness:** Their strong convictions can sometimes become inflexible, making it challenging to consider alternative viewpoints.
- **Unpredictability:** Their unconventional nature can sometimes manifest as unpredictability, which can be intriguing and confusing for those around them.

Despite their many strengths, Aquarians also face specific weaknesses that stem from their independent and forward-thinking nature. One notable weakness is their tendency to be emotionally detached. While this detachment allows them to approach situations objectively, it can sometimes hinder their ability to form deep emotional connections with others. This aloofness can be misconstrued as a lack of empathy or interest, potentially impacting their personal relationships.

Another area where Aquarians struggle is their stubbornness, especially regarding their beliefs and ideas. They often have strong convictions, and changing their mind can be difficult. This inflexibility can sometimes limit their perspective and hinder their ability to compromise or consider alternative viewpoints.

Aquarians' innovative and unconventional thinking, while a strength, can also lead to isolation or misunderstanding. Their ideas are often ahead of their time; not everyone may be ready or willing to embrace them. This can result in feelings of loneliness or frustration for Aquarians.

Their strong sense of independence can sometimes veer into a reluctance to accept help or collaborate closely with others.

Aquarians may prefer to work on their own terms, which can be challenging in team environments where cooperation and interdependence are crucial.

Aquarians can sometimes be unpredictable in their actions and decisions, driven by their desire for change and novelty. While this unpredictability can be exciting, it can also be disconcerting for those who prefer stability and consistency.

Aquarius's challenges – emotional detachment, stubbornness, feeling misunderstood, excessive independence, and unpredictability – reflect their innovative and autonomous nature. Recognizing and managing these aspects can help Aquarians find a more balanced approach to their interactions and endeavors.

Relationship Dynamics in Love and Friendship

- **Ideal Partners:** Those who appreciate Aquarius's originality and share their intellectual and humanitarian interests, like fellow Air signs Gemini and Libra or Fire signs like Aries and Leo.
- **Friendship Dynamics:** Aquarians seek open-minded, intellectually stimulating friends who support their unconventional ideas and social causes.

Aquarians, known for their originality and intellectualism, seek relationships that offer mental stimulation, shared humanitarian values, and respect for independence. Their approach to love and friendships is characterized by a desire for intellectual companionship, a shared interest in social issues, and a mutual respect for personal freedom.

Aquarians are thoughtful and caring partners in romantic relationships who value deep intellectual connections. They are drawn to open-minded, communicative partners who share their vision for a better world. However, Aquarians also value their independence and need a partner who understands their need for personal space and freedom.

In friendships, Aquarians are loyal and supportive. They seek friends who are intellectually stimulating and who share their unconventional interests. They enjoy friendships based on mutual interests in innovation, creativity, and social change. Their friends appreciate their visionary outlook and their commitment to making a difference.

Most Compatible Signs with Aquarius:

Gemini: This Air sign pairing is successful due to their mutual love for intellectual exploration and social interaction. Both Aquarius and Gemini are communicative, open-minded, and enjoy philosophical debates. Their mutual understanding of each other's need for freedom and variety creates a dynamic and stimulating relationship.

Libra: Another Air sign, Libra complements Aquarius's visionary nature with its charm and balance. This pairing is successful because both signs value social harmony, intellectual discussions, and artistic pursuits. Libra's diplomatic nature can help balance Aquarius's radical ideas, creating a harmonious and progressive partnership.

Aries: As a Fire sign, Aries brings passion and energy to the relationship, complementing Aquarius's intellectualism. This pairing is successful because Aries's enthusiasm and Aquarius's innovative ideas create a dynamic and exciting partnership. Both signs appreciate each other's independence and unique perspectives, building a relationship of growth and adventure.

Aquarius's compatibility in love and friendships revolves around intellectual connection, shared values, and respect for each other's autonomy. Relationships that offer mental stimulation, freedom, and a shared vision for the future will likely thrive with an Aquarian.

Career Insights

- **Career Paths:** Roles that allow for creative thinking, innovation, and social impact, such as technology, science, social work, or the arts.
- **In the Workplace:** Aquarians bring fresh perspectives and original ideas, often pushing the boundaries of conventional thinking.
- **Professional Development:** Embracing emotional intelligence and flexibility can enhance Aquarius's career growth and interpersonal relationships.

With their innovative mindset and humanitarian spirit, Aquarians bring a unique attitude to their professional lives. Their approach to work and career is often characterized by a desire for intellectual stimulation, creativity, and making a positive impact on society. They thrive in environments that value originality, offer intellectual challenges, and promote social change.

One of Aquarius's greatest strengths in the workplace is their ability to think outside the box. Their innovative approach to problem-solving often leads to unique and practical solutions. They excel in roles that require creative thinking and are not constrained by traditional methodologies.

Their strong sense of social justice and desire to contribute to the greater good make them effective in social change or community work roles. Aquarians are driven not just by personal success but also by the impact they can have on society.

However, Aquarians may sometimes need help with routine or highly structured environments. Their need for independence and variety can be at odds with conventional work settings. Embracing roles that offer flexibility and autonomy can enhance their job satisfaction.

Most Suitable Work/Career Choices for Aquarius:

Innovation or Technology: Aquarians' love for innovation and technology makes them well-suited for careers in these fields. Their ability to envision future trends and create groundbreaking technologies aligns perfectly with roles in tech startups, research and development, or digital innovation.

Social Work or Humanitarian Aid: Aquarians' humanitarian spirit and desire to make a difference in the world make them effective in social work, non-profit organizations, or humanitarian aid. They are driven by a passion to help others **and bring about social change.**

Creative Arts or Design: With their originality and creative flair, Aquarians excel in the arts or design fields. Whether in graphic design, fashion, or the performing arts, they bring a unique perspective that often sets new trends and pushes creative boundaries.

Science or Research: Aquarians' intellectual curiosity and analytical skills suit them for careers in science or research. They thrive in settings where they can explore new ideas, test theories, and contribute to advancing knowledge.

Entrepreneurship: Aquarians' independence and innovative thinking are critical assets in entrepreneurship. They excel in creating and leading ventures challenging the status quo and introducing new concepts or products.

Aquarians bring creativity, innovation, and a desire for social impact to their work and career. They excel in professions that allow them to utilize their visionary ideas, contribute to societal progress, and operate in environments that embrace unconventional thinking.

Famous Aquarius Personalities

- **Oprah Winfrey:** Embodies Aquarius's humanitarian spirit and innovative approach to media and communication.
- **Thomas Edison:** Reflects the inventiveness and intellectualism characteristic of Aquarius.
- **Ellen DeGeneres:** Represents Aquarius's social awareness, originality, and ability to connect with diverse audiences.

Aquarius brings a blend of innovation and humanitarianism to the zodiac. Their forward-thinking approach and strong sense of individuality fuel progressive ideas and social changes, making them impactful in both personal and professional spheres with their unique vision and altruistic spirit.

Chapter 14
PISCES

A Pisces swims effortlessly between reality and fantasy, often blurring the lines.

D ive into the enchanting world of Pisces, the zodiac's symbol of empathy and creativity. In this chapter, we explore the depths of Pisces, represented by the two fish. Pisceans are the artists and dreamers of the zodiac, known for their imagination, sensitivity, and emotional richness. If you're a Pisces, these pages will resonate with your intuitive and artistic spirit. For those who aren't, this chapter offers a glimpse into the mystical and emotional world of Pisces. From their profound creative expression to their deep emotional understanding, we'll uncover what makes these Water signs the embodiment of creativity and empathy.

Zodiac Birth Dates

February 19 - March 20: The period when the sun is in Pisces, bringing forth a time of heightened intuition, emotional sensitivity, and artistic inspiration.

Core Attributes

- **Ruling Planets:** Neptune and Jupiter, endowing Pisces with imaginative, dreamy qualities and a philosophical outlook.
- **Element:** Water, contributing to their emotional depth, intuition, and adaptability.
- **Symbol- The Two Fish:** Symbolizing Pisces's fluid and adaptable nature and their ability to navigate both the material and emotional realms.

Pisces is a sign of profound empathy, artistic talent, and an otherworldly intuition. Its symbol of two fish swimming in opposite directions marks Pisces' fluidity and adaptability. Pisces' ruling planet is Neptune, the planet of dreams and mysticism. Pisceans are naturally drawn to the abstract and the transcendent, often attuned to realms beyond the tangible.

As a Water sign, Pisces is deeply connected to the emotional undercurrents of life. They navigate the world with a compassionate heart, often acting as a sponge for the feelings of those around them. This deep emotional capacity allows them to relate to others with unparalleled understanding.

The dual fish symbolizes the constant pull between fantasy and reality that defines the Pisces experience. This duality equips them to adapt and flow with life's changing tides, sometimes confusing them about where their feelings end, and others begin.

Pisces are known for their boundless creativity. Their imaginative prowess is often channeled into artistic expression through painting, music, writing, or dance. Their artistry is a form of personal enjoyment and communicates their rich inner life and profound insights.

The core attributes of Pisces—compassion, artistic inclination, intuition, emotional depth, and adaptability—create a personality that is at once nurturing and enigmatic, capable of profound connection and artistic expression.

Personality Traits

- **Empathetic and Intuitive:** Pisceans have a natural talent to understand and connect with the emotions of others, often feeling deeply attuned to people's needs and feelings.
- **Creative and Artistic:** With a rich imagination, Pisceans often express themselves through various art forms, finding solace and expression in creativity.

- **Dreamy and Reflective:** They usually have a contemplative nature, spending time in their inner world of emotions and thoughts, exploring the depths of their psyche.

Pisceans are known for a constellation of personality traits that reflect their deep emotional world and creative minds. One of the most defining traits is their empathy. Pisceans have an innate ability to understand and share the feelings of others, often sensing emotions as if they were their own. This makes them exceptionally compassionate and caring individuals.

Creativity flows through Pisces as naturally as Water. Their vivid imagination and artistic sensibilities find outlets in every form of creative expression. Whether through painting, music, or story-telling, Pisceans have a unique way of capturing and communicating the subtleties of human experience.

They are also dreamers, often lost in their own thoughts and fantasies. This dreaminess is a double-edged sword—the source of their creativity and intuition. Still, it can also lead them to a tendency to escape into their own inner world, avoiding the harsher realities of life.

Pisceans are known for their adaptability, able to flow with the circumstances like the Water that represents their sign. They can be remarkably flexible in their thoughts and behaviors, which often helps them gracefully navigate life's more turbulent waters.

At the same time, this fluid nature can sometimes lead to a lack of boundaries and a tendency to conform to the energies and desires of others, losing sight of their own needs and identity.

Intuitive and often psychic, Pisceans seem to have an innate understanding of the universe's unseen threads, connecting them deeply to the spiritual and metaphysical aspects of existence.

In essence, the personality of a Pisces is a blend of empathetic depth, artistic brilliance, dreamy contemplation, and intuitive insight, all woven together with an adaptable and mutable spirit.

Innate Strengths

- **Emotional Intelligence:** Pisceans have high emotional intelligence, enabling them to navigate complex dynamic landscapes with empathy and understanding.
- **Creativity:** Their imaginative and artistic abilities are profound, often leading them to excel in creative fields where they can express their inner visions.
- **Adaptability:** Pisceans are highly adaptable and able to adjust to different situations and people easily, reflecting their mutable water nature.

Pisceans boast many strengths stemming from their empathetic nature and rich imagination. One of their most admirable strengths is their profound empathy. This allows them to connect with others deeply emotionally and offer genuine compassion and understanding. Their ability to empathize often makes them the confidants and counselors in their social circles.

Creativity is another hallmark of the Pisces personality. Their imaginative minds are constantly brimming with ideas and visions, which they can channel into artistic endeavors or creative solutions to problems. Whether through art, writing, or music, Pisceans have a natural talent for expressing the nuances of the human experience.

Pisceans are also incredibly adaptable. Like the Water that symbolizes their sign, they can shape themselves to fit the contours of any situation, making them flexible and versatile. This adaptability allows them to navigate life's unpredictable waters with resilience and grace.

Their intuition is robust, giving them insight into situations and people others might miss. Pisceans seem to have an internal compass that guides them through their interactions and decisions, even if they can't always explain their reasons logically.

Pisces' gentle and caring nature often inspires trust and loyalty in others. Pisceans are known for making people feel seen and heard, which endears them to friends and colleagues.

The strengths of Pisces – empathy, creativity, adaptability, intuition, and gentleness – make them deeply connected and creative individuals. They are often the healing and artistic forces in their communities, bringing comfort and inspiration to those around them.

Challenges to Overcome

- **Over-sensitivity:** Their deep empathy can sometimes lead to over-sensitivity, making them vulnerable to the emotional states of others.
- **Tendency to Escape Reality:** Their dreamy nature can sometimes result in escapism, where they might avoid confronting harsher realities.
- **Indecisiveness:** Pisceans sometimes struggle to make firm decisions, especially when they feel pulled in different emotional directions.

Although intuitive and compassionate, Pisces has weaknesses that can pose challenges. One of the primary weaknesses is their tendency toward over-sensitivity. While their deep empathy allows them to connect with others, it can also leave them vulnerable to being deeply affected by the moods and troubles of those around them, sometimes to their detriment.

Their dreamy and reflective nature, a wellspring for their creativity, can also lead to escapism. Pisces may find themselves retreating into their inner world as a coping mechanism, avoiding the less pleasant aspects of reality rather than confronting or addressing them directly.

Indecisiveness can also be a stumbling block for Pisces. Their ability to see multiple sides of every issue is a strength. Still, it can leave them floating in a sea of uncertainty, struggling to commit to a course of action, especially when their emotions are pulled in various directions.

Additionally, their desire to help and to heal can sometimes cross into the realm of self-sacrifice. Pisces might have difficulty setting boundaries, often putting others' needs before their own and potentially neglecting their well-being.

Their mutable nature, while contributing to their adaptability, can sometimes manifest as a lack of direction. Pisces may drift along without a clear plan, making it challenging to achieve their goals or make tangible progress in their personal and professional lives.

Pisces can be prone to idealism, sometimes viewing the world through rose-colored glasses. Disappointment can result when reality falls short of their lofty expectations.

The challenges facing Pisces – over-sensitivity, escapism, indecisiveness, tendency towards self-sacrifice, lack of direction, and idealism – are reflections of their deep empathy and imaginative spirit. Recognizing and managing these aspects can help Pisces find a healthier balance and navigate the world more effectively.

Relationship Dynamics in Love and Friendships

- **Ideal Partners:** Those who understand Pisces's emotional depth and appreciate their creativity, such as fellow Water signs Cancer and Scorpio or Earth signs like Taurus and Capricorn.
- **Friendship Dynamics:** Pisceans seek empathetic, creative friends who share their depth of feeling and artistic interests.

With their deep well of empathy and artistic soul, Pisces navigates the waters of love and friendship with a blend of emotional depth and creative flair. In personal relationships, they seek connections that resonate with their profound understanding and appreciation for life's mystical and romantic aspects.

Pisces are nurturing, sensitive, and often selflessly devoted in romantic partnerships. They desire partners who understand their profound emotional nature and share their appreciation for life's subtler, more poetic aspects. For Pisces, love is not just an emotion but an artistic and spiritual journey.

Friendships for Pisces are often marked by a strong emotional bond. They are the friends who will empathize with you, offer a shoulder to lean on and share your joys and sorrows with equal intensity. They value friends who appreciate their dreamy nature and can join them in exploring both the creative and spiritual realms.

Most Compatible Signs with Pisces:

Cancer: Both being Water signs, Pisces and Cancer share a profound emotional understanding. This pairing is successful due to their mutual empathy, desire for deep emotional connections, and shared love for home and family. Together, they create a nurturing and harmonious relationship, providing each other with the emotional security they crave.

Scorpio: Scorpio brings an intensity and depth to the relationship that complements Pisces' empathetic nature. Both signs share a love for life's mystical and unspoken emotional undercurrents. Their deep, transformative, and intensely inspirational connection makes for a passionate and enduring bond.

Taurus: Taurus provides the stability and practicality to ground Pisces' sometimes ethereal nature. This relationship is successful because Taurus offers the solid foundation Pisces needs. At the same time, Pisces brings a sense of romance and creativity. They balance each other out together, creating an imaginative and down-to-earth relationship.

In summary, Pisces finds the most harmonious relationships with signs offering emotional depth, intuitive understanding, and a mystical touch. Their ideal partnerships balance emotional support, creative inspiration, and stability.

Career Insights

- **Career Paths:** Roles that allow for creative expression, emotional connection, and helping others, such as the arts, counseling, or healthcare.
- **In the Workplace:** Pisceans bring creativity, empathy, and a collaborative spirit, often contributing a unique

perspective and emotional intelligence.
- **Professional Development**: Focusing on practical skills and decision-making can enhance Pisces's career growth and effectiveness in achieving their goals.

Pisces bring a unique blend of empathy, creativity, and intuition to their professional lives. Their approach to work and career is often influenced by their desire to find meaning and emotional satisfaction in what they do. They are well-suited to jobs that allow them to express their artistic talents, help others, or explore the depths of their own or others' psyches.

One of Pisces' greatest strengths in the workplace is their imaginative approach. They excel in roles that allow them to dream and create, bringing innovation and a fresh perspective to their projects. Their empathy makes them excellent team players who are sensitive to the needs and feelings of their colleagues, fostering a harmonious work environment.

Their intuitive nature can also be a significant asset. Pisces often have a gut feeling about a project or decision's direction, and their insights can be surprisingly accurate. Their ability to understand and work with subtle energies can make them invaluable in roles that require a nuanced approach.

However, Pisces may sometimes struggle with work's more mundane or administrative aspects. Their dislike for routine and their need for a deeper connection with their work can lead to dissatisfaction with jobs that are too structured or lack creative freedom.

Most Suitable Work/Career Choices for Pisces:

Arts and Creative Fields: Pisces' natural creativity and artistic skills are well-utilized in the arts. Whether as painters, musicians, writers, or actors, they can channel their rich inner worlds into beautiful and profound creative expressions.

Healthcare and Healing Professions: Pisces' empathy and desire to help make them suited for careers in healthcare, whether as doctors, nurses, therapists, or counselors. Their compassion and intuitive understanding of human emotion provide comfort and healing to those in need.

Social Work: With their strong sense of compassion and social justice, Pisces can find great satisfaction in social work. They are driven to make a difference in the lives of others, and their ability to empathize with diverse populations makes them effective in this field.

Spiritual or Religious Work: Pisces' deep spiritual insight and interest in the metaphysical can lead them to careers as spiritual leaders, counselors, or in other roles within religious or spiritual communities where they can guide and support others on their spiritual journeys.

Marine Biology or Environmental Science: Their affinity for Water and the life within it can draw Pisces to careers related to marine biology or environmental science, where they can work to understand and protect the oceans and waterways that inspire them.

Pisces excels in work and jobs that allow them to leverage their creativity, empathy, and intuition strengths. They thrive in environments that provide emotional and artistic fulfillment and the opportunity to positively impact the world or individual lives.

Famous Pisces Personalities

- **Albert Einstein:** Reflects Pisces's intuitive mind and philosophical nature.
- **Rihanna:** Embodies the creativity, empathy, and artistic expression characteristic of Pisces.
- **Steve Jobs:** Demonstrates Pisces's imaginative vision and ability to transform ideas into reality.

Pisces embodies empathy and creativity within the zodiac. Their deep emotional understanding and artistic flair enrich relationships and environments, making them compassionate confidants and imaginative contributors in both personal and professional realms.

Stars Aligning: Your Review Lights the Way
Share Your Journey, Illuminate Another's Path

Congratulations! You've journeyed through the cosmic tapestry of "Astrology for Beginners: A Simple Zodiac Guide to Understand the 12 Star Signs and Unlock Self-Discovery, Personality Traits, and Compatibility." Armed with the insights and knowledge about the stars above, you're now equipped to navigate life with a bit more understanding of yourself and those around you.

But the journey doesn't end here. The universe is vast, and its secrets are endless, much like the potential for discovery within each of us. Now, it's your turn to be the guiding light for someone else embarking on their own journey of self-discovery and cosmic exploration.

Here's how you can share your thoughts and keep the cycle of learning and growth going:

Reflect on Your Experience: Think about how this book has opened your eyes to the stars. Did you uncover something new about yourself? Did it change the way you view others?

Write a Review: Take a moment to share your reflections. Your review doesn't have to be as elaborate as the constellations; simple, heartfelt thoughts are perfect. By sharing your insights, you're not just leaving feedback; you're providing a beacon for others who are just starting to navigate the zodiac.

Pass It On: If this book has sparked a newfound appreciation for astrology in you, consider sharing it with someone else who's curious about the stars. Whether it's a friend, a family member, or even someone you've just met, your recommendation could be the nudge they need to start their own celestial journey.

To leave your review, simply scan the QR code below:

Your voice matters more than you might think. In a universe filled with countless stars, each review is like a light shining brightly, guiding others to discover the wonders of astrology. You've gained valuable insights from the stars; now, it's time to help others do the same.

Thank you for being a part of this cosmic journey. May the stars continue to guide you and inspire curiosity and wonder in your heart.

- Your fellow star navigator, Honey Barnes

PS - Remember, every shared experience is like a star twinkling in the night sky, making the path clearer for someone else. Your review is a gift that keeps on giving, illuminating the way for countless others.

Conclusion
Continuing Your Astrological Journey

As we conclude our celestial exploration in "Astrology for Beginners," we have journeyed through the twelve signs of the zodiac, each an intricate tapestry of traits, strengths, and nuances that contribute to the rich mosaic of human experience. From the pioneering spirit of Aries to the compassionate depths of Pisces, astrology offers a unique lens through which to view ourselves and others.

We've learned that astrology is not just about sun signs but a complex and interconnected system that mirrors the complexities of life itself. Each sign, with its elements and modalities, paints a distinctive picture of personality, compatibility, and potential paths in life. We've seen how the fiery ambition of Leo can illuminate our courage while the earthy pragmatism of Taurus can ground our dreams in reality. We've discovered the air sign's intellectual spark in Aquarius and the emotional tides that flow through the water sign of Cancer.

This book is merely the beginning of what can be a lifelong journey. For those eager to dive deeper into the cosmic ocean of astrology, the following steps involve exploring your own birth chart—an astrological snapshot of the skies at the moment of your birth. This chart is a personal guide, rich with insights into not just your sun sign but your moon sign, rising sign, and planet positions that all contribute to the unique individual you are.

For those of you who found resonance, inspiration, or curiosity within these pages, I encourage you to continue exploring. Astrology offers tools for self-discovery and reflection, providing a framework to better understand our traits, behaviors, and tendencies.

Suppose this guide has provided new insights or sparked a deeper interest in astrology. In that case, I invite you to share your thoughts and experiences. Your reviews on Amazon support the book and join the collective conversation on astrology, helping others on their path to self-discovery.

Astrology is a journey, not a destination. As you continue to navigate the celestial currents, may the stars illuminate your path to deeper understanding and growth.

Resources

Throughout "Astrology for Beginners," we've drawn upon a wealth of astrological knowledge and resources to create an accessible guide for those starting their journey into the zodiac. Below is a reference section for further exploration and to credit the sources that have illuminated our path:

- Parker, Julia, and Derek Parker. "The Complete Astrologer." A comprehensive guide covering all aspects of Western astrology, including historical context and modern interpretations. Parker, D., & Parker, J. (1971). *The Compleat Astrologer.* McGraw-Hill Companies.
- Hall, Judy. "The Astrology Bible: The Definitive Guide to the Zodiac." An extensive resource that delves into each zodiac sign, and the planets and houses offer insights into how they influence personality and life events. Hall, J. (2005). *The Astrology Bible: The Definitive Guide to the Zodiac. Sterling Publishing Company, Inc.*
- Arroyo, Stephen. "Astrology, Psychology, and the Four Elements: An Energy Approach to Astrology & Its Use in the Counseling Arts." This book provides an in-depth look at the psychological underpinnings of astrological elements and how they interact with human behavior and experiences. Arroyo, S. (2012). *Astrology, psychology and the four Elements: An Energy Approach to Astrology & Its Use in the Counselling Arts.* Motilal Banarsidass.

- Forrest, Steven. "The Inner Sky: How to Make Wiser Choices for a More Fulfilling Life." Steven Forrest introduces the concept of evolutionary astrology and how it can be used to make informed choices for personal growth. Forrest, S. (2012). *The inner sky: How to Make Wiser Choices for a More Fulfilling Life*. Seven Paws PressInc.
- Woolfolk, Joanna Martine. "The Only Astrology Book You'll Ever Need." A popular reference for beginners, covering everything from understanding your birth chart to predictions and compatibility. Woolfolk, J. M. (2012). *The only astrology book you'll ever need: Now with an Interactive PC- and Mac-Compatible CD*. Taylor Trade Publications.
- OpenAI's ChatGPT: As the author and compiler of "Astrology for Beginners," OpenAI's ChatGPT has synthesized astrological concepts into a digestible format suitable for newcomers. The outputs provided in this book, including the conclusion chapter and other sections, are original content generated by OpenAI's ChatGPT, accessible as of April 2023.

For readers who wish to delve deeper into astrology, these references offer a solid foundation for further study and exploration. These resources will provide valuable guidance if you want to understand your personal astrology or the broader philosophical implications.

27041503R00108